HOW TO DO

ACCENTS

Edda Sharpe & Jan Haydn Rowles

OBERON BOOKS
LONDON

First published in 2007 by Oberon Books Ltd
521 Caledonian Road, London N7 9RH
Tel: +44 (0) 20 7607 3637 / Fax: +44 (0) 20 7607 3629
e-mail: info@oberonbooks.com
www.oberonbooks.com

Second edition (revised), 2009

Reprinted with corrections and additional sample accent tracks in 2012, 2015, 2016, 2017, 2018

Printed and bound by CPI Group (UK) Ltd, Croydon, CR0 4YY.

Visit www.oberonbooks.com to read more about all our books and to buy them. You will also find features, author interviews and news of any author events, and you can sign up for e-newsletters so that you're always first to hear about our new releases.

HOW TO DO ACCENTS

CONTENTS

ACKNOWLEDGEMENTS AND THANKS

For their help with the making of this book we would like to thank: Arsher Ali, Laura Caroll, Kevin Coe, Steve Cooper, Trevor Cuthbertson (also one of our test readers), Sid Dixon, Louise Dolan, Katie Draper, Joanna Gaskell, Darren Halley, Wilbur Heynes, Donna Humphries, Dylan Kennedy, Martin Larmour, David Lyons, Jor'el Mitchell (also one of our test readers), Channelle Owen, Catrin Picand-Jones, Nora Ryan Taylor, for their accent samples; Matt Walters at Quince Studios; Rachel Williams, Mariele Runacre-Temple and Gill Sharpe for the drawings and illustrations; our test readers, including Richard Ryder and Julie Legrand, for their comments and input, and Professor Valerie Hazan (Professor of Speech Science and Head of the Department of Phonetics and Linguistics, University College London) for her input and advice.

A huge thank you to all past and present students of ours, especially to those at East 15 Acting School, who have continually deepened our understanding of working with actors; to all those professional actors and directors who have fed our passion over the years; and finally to all at Oberon, especially our editor Stephen Watson.

Jan would like to thank Lyn Darnley, Head of Voice at the RSC, Jeanette Nelson, Head of Voice at the National Theatre; good friends and colleagues, and other fellow voice teachers who have inspired and encouraged – Thanks also to friends and family for the regular 'check-ins'.

The biggest thanks to my very dear friend, colleague and fantastic co-writer Edda: thank you for the most fun-filled, laughter-led and inspirational times.

Edda would like to thank Jackie Maxwell, Christopher Newton and Neil Munro, of the Shaw Festival Theatre, Canada; David Willis, Sarah Shippobotham, Christina Gutekunst and John Gillett for their friendship, professional support and integrity; my friends and family, and of course, an enormous thank you to my very special friend and professional soulmate, Jan.

INTRODUCTION

HOW THIS BOOK CAME ABOUT

Acting with an accent can be a dream or a nightmare for an actor. The pressures to get it right – to sound authentic, honest and connected – grow as audiences become more demanding and the world gets smaller.

In *How to Do Accents* we offer actors a new approach. Speaking with an accent is a skill just like any other: it can be learned and developed, and it is our aim with this book to provide you with the tools to do just that.

Actors sometimes get the feeling that before they can approach an accent they must understand the phonetic alphabet. Although this approach provides some people with a sense of security, it deals with only a small part of what makes up an accent. Moreover, the vast majority of actors find this approach at best alienating and at worst simply boring. Unfortunately this can lead them to ignore the essential structure inherent in accents, believing this leaves them free to learn on a more intuitive level. The results are accents that are extremely hit and miss to begin with, and once the actor's emotions kick in the accent flies out of the window. It simply isn't in their muscle memory, and how can it be? Intuition is essential, but so is structure. The very word 'structure' may be causing you to glaze over, but, if you think about it, it is hardly an alien concept to actors. They use it every day in their craft. They learn the structure of lines, of moves, even the structure of emotions. The structure of accents can be part of this: it simply needs to be accessible.

What is desperately needed is a simple, reassuring system for both learning and teaching accents: a system that allows the actor to use their gift for intuition in tandem with their ability to retain structure; a system that liberates the nervous while developing the skills of the keen; a system that teaches actors not just one accent, but the underlying structure inherent in *all* accents. This book provides such a system.

Using solid technical know-how, clear practical steps, real-life examples, and the occasional dose of humour, the Haydn/Sharpe System brings to the surface the underlying structure of accents, sharing the processes that we, as specialist dialect coaches, have developed, to give you the insight, tools and confidence to work with *any* accent.

WHAT THIS BOOK IS NOT...

This is not a linguistic or phonetic textbook, but it is completely compatible with them. We have taken the language of the linguist and translated it into the language of the actor. We have distilled the very detailed work of phoneticians and extracted the elements relevant to the specific goals of the actor at work.

So who's this book for?

- The drama student
- The actor working with accents and dialect coaches
- The voice and dialect teacher
- The drama teacher
- Anyone who's ever wondered *How to Do Accents*!

WHAT'S IN THIS BOOK

1   **Get started** (page 19)

This chapter covers the preparation needed in order to build your new accent successfully:

- Knowing your equipment.
- Making and using a resource recording.
- Establishing the cultural context of an accent.

2   **The Foundations** (page 27)

This chapter takes you through the four essential elements needed for a solid accent *foundation*:

- **The Setting** – The setting of the muscles of the face and mouth.
- **The Zone** – Where the sound is placed.
- **The Tone** – The resonant quality of the accent.
- **The Direction** – The direction in which the voice is sent.

3   **The Two Planets** (Rhotic vs. Non-Rhotic) (page 39)

In this chapter you will discover that when it comes to accents the world divides into two planets:

- **Planet Rhotic,** where people say an R *whenever* it is written.
- **Planet Non-Rhotic,** where people *only* say an R if there is a vowel sound *spoken* after it.

More significantly you'll discover which planet you're on, and how to pass as a local on the other!

4   **The Bite** (page 55)

Consonants break the flow of the voice into Bite-size pieces. In this chapter we will lead you through:

- 5 **Major Players** – that have the power to make or break your accent.
- 3 **Major Issues** – that can affect any consonant and change the quality of an accent.
- **Springing Consonants** – consonants in vowel's clothing.
- **'YOO'** – a small detail just waiting to catch you out!

5   **The Shapes** (page 113)

This chapter shows you how to establish the vowel shapes of an accent. You will discover a spectrum of possibilities in your mouth through:

- **Getting the Big Picture** – how to use a word list.

- **Inventories and Distributions** – what are the shapes and where do they go?

- **Shape, Length and Movement** – what to listen for to identify changes in vowels.

- **Getting more Detailed** – watching out for environmental issues.

6 **The Groove** (page 149)

Every accent has its own music, made up from the interplay of rhythms and intonation patterns, that we call the Groove. In this chapter we show you how to give your accent depth and roots through:

- **The Big Picture** – framing and embodying the cultural and physical dynamics inherent in the Groove.

- **Intonation** – refining our ear to the essentials of rhythm, melody and meaning.

7 **Get Professional** (page 165)

In this chapter we show you how to take your accent to a professional level with advice on how to:

- **Get Practising**

And what to do when your accent meets the demands of a:

- **Production**
- **Character**
- **Audition**

8 **Useful Stuff** (page 175)

This chapter covers the following:

- **Making a Resource Recording** – The KIT LIST, the Set Text 'Arthur the Rat', Major Player Elicitation sentences, Free Speech prompts.

- **You and the New Charts** – An example of one we did earlier, plus a blank chart for you to fill in.

- **Knowing your Equipment** – Lips and cheeks, jaw, tongue, soft palate, voice box.

- **Space Exploration** – the Vowel Spectrum chart, Exploration and discovery of the eight extreme vowels.

HOW TO USE THIS BOOK

You can use this book to work on a specific accent or to learn the structure inherent in *all* accents, using your own resource material and/or the downloadable tracks provided. You may want to work through the book systematically, working step by step through the different elements. Or perhaps you are someone who likes to dip in and out of books when the need arises, picking out the relevant bits and getting a good overview. Either way this book will work for you.

If you are learning…

● **the structures inherent in ALL accents**

This book provides you with a complete course in how to do accents. By working through the book and listening to the tracks you will understand the structures and develop the skills to be able to do not just one accent, but *any* accent.

If you are learning…

● **a SPECIFIC accent**

Look at the example You and the New chart on page 182 to see how it works and then use the:

● blank **You and the New chart** (page 192)

● resource recording (either your own or one of the sample accents we provide on tracks 84-100, or download The ACCENT Kit app: ios bit.ly/U9jZNL & Android bit.ly/12nSrIq)

● checklists (pages 38, 52, 65, 72, 76, 81, 87, 94, 100, 106, 112, 121, 131, 133, 140, 148, 164)

to build up a complete profile of the structure and patterns of your new accent.

We have broken the architecture of accents into five areas: **The Foundations**; **The Two Planets**; **The Bite**; **The Shapes**; and **The Groove**. These define the principal points of change from one accent to another. By necessity we have used a limited selection of accents as our examples, but the patterns demonstrated will apply to any accent of English. Recognising patterns, knowing the limited options available to your accent and having a simple structure for remembering them are all key to being able to do an accent.

Whether you are using *How to Do Accents* as a work book to develop your understanding of how accents work, or to build up the profile of a specific accent, it is best to take one area of the work at a time. Give your brain time to absorb new information and to get used to the new way of interpreting and creating sound. Working steadily for half an hour or so a day can be better than doing two solid hours once a week. Where possible, find the pace that works for you.

Sensing

Being good at accents is about so much more than 'having a good ear'. It is about using *all* your available senses to learn new skills, just as you did as a small child. For this reason we encourage you throughout the book to **see, feel** and **hear** new accents.

Through the book you will see these icons:

 This icon prompts you to focus in a **visual** way, either by looking at an illustration, using your mind's eye, or looking in a mirror.

 This icon prompts you to focus on **physical** processes and feelings.

 This icon prompts you to focus in an **aural** way by listening to a track on the downloadable MP3s. See page 224 for instructions on how to download the tracks that accompany the book.

 This icon also prompts you to focus in an **aural** way by listening to yourself.

Creating a Funnel

When learning new sounds it helps to have a way of listening to yourself that is instant and gives you an accurate 'outside ear' on the sounds you are making. You can do this by 'funnelling' the sound from your mouth straight back to your ear.

Put one hand about five centimetres (two inches) away from your mouth, cup it onto the bottom of the other hand which then in turn cups behind the ear, creating a funnel from one to the other.

You will know you've got the position right when you hear your voice loud and clear, even when you are speaking quietly. This is especially invaluable when you are working in a group, or when you need to practise quietly.

Practising

When you were a child you dedicated hours to hearing the sounds, and/or seeing the shapes of the faces around you, playing with the shape of your mouth, until the sounds and shapes *you* were making matched the sounds and shapes you were *hearing* and/or *seeing*. Then you practised those shapes and movements over and over again until they became locked into your muscle memory. That's what children do. That's what you did and how you learned to speak. That's why you have an accent, even if you think you don't!

For some of you, your mimicry instinct may still be active – maybe you've always enjoyed playing with new sounds – while others of you may have turned it off long ago, happy to sound like those around you. Whichever you are, prepare to switch your mimicry instinct back on and practise as hard as a child!

Remember, learning how to do accents is just like anything else you've successfully learnt: riding a bike, speaking a language, or even navigating a new mobile phone. Some things seem to come easily; others seem to take longer to get into the muscle memory. Separate out the different elements, identify what you know, recognise what you don't know and then learn, re-learn and above all *practise*. During this process your awareness is very high and the focus and juggling can seem complicated. Don't panic – this just means there is more learning taking place! Soon the elements come together and the process seems natural and effortless.

Processing

To help you teach your left brain (where logic and structure live) to store the discoveries you are making, the Haydn/Sharpe System provides you with two invaluable tools.

● **You and the New**

One thing that will really help you to do *other* accents is understanding your *own*. By building a profile of the qualities specific to your own accent you can establish a solid base from which to navigate other accents.

If you look towards the back of the book (pages 192–201), you will see a chart called **You and the New**. You will be prompted at the end of each chapter to fill it in. Once filled in, this will provide you with an instant comparison between your accent and the new accents you are working on, showing you where the most significant changes are. Photocopy this before you start, as you may want to use it each time you learn a new accent. (Alternatively, you can download the chart as a ready-to-print pdf from the *How to Do Accents* website at **www.howtodoaccents.com**.)

● **Checklists**

At the end of each chapter we have provided a checklist of the elements you will be looking out for in any new accent. Use these to be sure you leave no stone unturned in your search for an authentic, detailed accent.

Learning an accent is all about layering. Take it a piece at a time, practise all the pieces and then put them all together. And above all be prepared to make mistakes and sound silly: this is just you and your brain learning!

1

GET STARTED

IN THIS CHAPTER...

We introduce you to three areas that you need to be on top of before you begin work on any accent:

1 **Knowing your equipment.** Accents are physical. They are made by your body. In order to adapt you will need to have some basic knowledge of the physical equipment you have and how it works. In this section we introduce you to those basics.

2 **Making and using a Resource Recording.** One essential practical requirement when learning a new accent is a resource recording. You cannot learn an accent out of thin air. In this section we show you how to find, make and use a resource recording to get the most from yourself and this book!

3 **Getting into the Scene.** Accents don't exist in a vacuum. They are made by living, breathing communities, subject to the vagaries of history, politics, peer pressure, climate, culture, economics and more. You name it: somewhere along the line external influences have had and continue to have an effect on the way we speak. Contextualising your accent is a vital step towards owning it and making it real.

If you are about to study a specific accent make sure you have the following before you start:

1 A good resource recording of the accent.

2 A recording device that you can also play back on.

3 A mirror.

4 A notebook.

5 This book. (Obviously.)

How to Do Accents

KNOWING YOUR EQUIPMENT

Our lips, jaw, tongue, soft palate and cheeks are always on the move, flicking, tapping, gliding and making contact with one another, dancing their way through thousands and thousands of different shapes and sounds, and yet we don't give it a second thought!

In order to understand how all these shapes and sounds are made it helps to be familiar with your own bits, the **Articulators,** and to know what the various parts are called, which part is being used, and how the various parts make contact.

In other words, to do accents you will need to know which *active* articulator is doing what with which *passive* articulator!

Throughout this book we will be using this simplified diagram of the articulators:

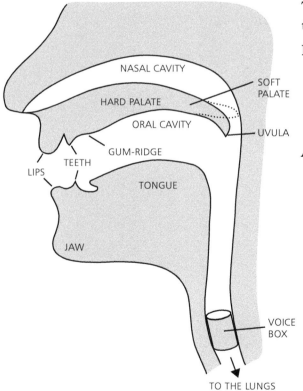

The articulators divide into two groups:

Passive (non-moving)

1   **Teeth**

2   **Upper gum-ridge**

3   **Hard palate**

Active (moving)

1   **Lips/cheeks**

2   **(Lower) Jaw**

3   **Tongue**

4   **Soft palate**

It may be that you already have a good understanding of all this, but if this is all new to you, or you feel in need of a refresher, go to 'Knowing Your Equipment', Useful Stuff, page 202.

WORKING WITH A RESOURCE RECORDING

In order to have something to mimic it is essential to have a good **resource recording**: a recorded example of at least one real speaker speaking in the accent you are looking to learn. (After all, children don't learn to speak in a vacuum!)

It's amazing the number of actors we meet who say, 'I've tried to do a Welsh accent (or Irish, or Newcastle, etc) and I'm rubbish!' – only to discover the only time they've ever actually *heard* it was when they went there on holiday ten years before. People have such high expectations of their poor old brains: they seem to expect to be able to do an accent without giving their eyes, ears and mouths a chance to really absorb and learn it. Give yourself a break. You could be brilliant if you had the right tools and practised in the right way!

 This book comes with downloadable tracks of 17 accents of English. You can find them on tracks 84-100. They are;

- *Norfolk* (TRACK 84)
- *Yorkshire* (TRACK 85)
- *Standard Canadian* (TRACK 86)
- *Standard Australian* (TRACK 87)
- *Standard American* (TRACK 88)
- *Northern Ireland/Belfast* (TRACK 89)
- *Southern Ireland/Cork* (TRACK 90)
- *Scottish/Glasgow* (TRACK 91)
- *Newcastle-upon-Tyne* (TRACK 92)
- *Manchester* (TRACK 93)
- *Liverpool* (TRACK 94)
- *South Wales/Swansea* (TRACK 95)
- *West Midlands/Walsall* (TRACK 96)
- *Cockney* (TRACK 97)
- *Neutral Standard English* (TRACK 98)
- *Contemporary 'Street' London* (TRACK 99)
- *Cornish* (TRACK 100)

If you want to learn a different accent from these you will need your own resource recording, and here's how to get one...

Making your own resource recording ───────

Sometimes the best way of getting what you want is to do it yourself. Here's how.

Find a willing candidate or candidates to record. Two examples are better than one, as you will then have more information to work from. Try places like cultural centres, universities, acting schools, embassies and tourist centres to find the people you want. Remember to be as specific about age, gender, cultural background, etc, as you can: these things can make a huge difference.

Here's what you will need:

- a portable recording device (it doesn't matter how up to date it is so long as it works!)
- the KIT LIST (see Useful Stuff, page 179)
- Major Player Elicitation sentences (see Useful Stuff, page 181)
- the Standard Text (see Useful Stuff, page 180)
- questions to elicit conversational speech (see Useful Stuff, page 181).

Practise using your recording device: it really doesn't help someone to be at their ease if you fumble about with microphones.

This may be obvious but…do a test to make sure it's recording! (Jan has several old dialect tapes with nothing on them because her pause button was still on.)

Make sure the device is next to *them* and not you. You want their voice, not your own! (Edda has many a tape from her early days where she is loud and clear and the person being interviewed can be heard faintly in the distance.)

Where to find existing resource recordings ───────

It is possible to find good commercial recordings, though they more than likely don't have the KIT LIST or Standard Text in them. There are plenty of helpful booklets with CDs on the market (Allyn Partin and Gillian Lane Plescia and Penny Dyer, for example, produce a wealth of good recordings with basic vowel information and native speakers) and this book will enable you to use those materials more successfully.

Needless to say, the internet is an invaluable resource. With good broadband facilities you can hear the sounds of the world, and, where copyright allows, even burn them onto your own CDs. We have given a list of some of the websites that we have found most useful in the Appendix (page 219).

How to listen to your resource recording ——————

Once you have found or made your recording there are ways and means of listening to it to get the best out of both it and you.

Unstructured listening

- To begin with, let yourself respond intuitively to get your juices flowing! You may well find yourself wanting to mimic immediately, so do. Always remember to encourage that instinct.

- Write down anything – and we mean *anything* – you notice: perhaps the tune strikes you first, maybe it sounds 'flat', or a bit 'choppy'; or perhaps you notice specific words, either because they are unusual words or because they say them in a very different way from you. You'll probably find you are noticing a lot in this unstructured way. As you work through this book you will be able to put these initial discoveries into the structure of your new accent.

- If you have a video or DVD recording you can also look at the shapes the speakers are making, how the mouth is held, how much the jaw, lips and cheeks move, or don't. These are all things worth noticing.

Structured listening

- Unstructured listening only kick-starts the process. What this book will show you is the next vital step: how to listen in a *structured* way.

- As you work through this book we will give you examples of specific sounds and combinations of sounds on the accompanying downloadable tracks. These are the sounds to listen for on your resource recording.

- Listen to the same phrase on your resource recording many times over for your ear to identify the element you are listening for, both for your mouth to accurately mimic it, and for your brain to retain it. Once simply won't be enough!

GET INTO THE SCENE

Accents don't exist in a vacuum. They are made by living, breathing communities, subject to the vagaries of history, politics, peer pressure, climate, culture, economics and more. Contextualising your accent is a vital step towards owning it and making it real. Remember, as the world gets smaller, authenticity becomes ever more important.

Putting it into a cultural and physical context ————

- It sounds obvious, but know where you are on the map! Everywhere exists in relation to somewhere else: you have to know your neighbours to know yourself (one of those clichés that happens to be true). When you see how close they are on the map it's hardly surprising that when you do a Newcastle accent you can sometimes sound Scottish. It can even be reassuring.

- Find out as much as you can about the music, dance, art and culture of an area. These influences may directly affect or indeed reflect the way people speak. Either way, immersing yourself in them helps you to feel the heartbeat of the people: think of Irish dancing and the rhythms of the bodhrán; Country and Western songs bending the notes on the sliding guitar; Yiddish klezmer music with its minor keys, fast trills and sliding notes (to name just a few significant examples).

- If you possibly can, visit the area. Nothing compares with being immersed in the accent, meeting the people and breathing in the landscape. If you can't get there, many organisations produce websites and tourist videos which can give you a flavour of the same experience.

- You may find cultural centres, organisations and community groups in your own area that have the accent you are looking for – for example, the London Welsh Centre or the New York Irish Centre. Visit them!

- We have to give a mention to the Wikipedia website. It is an incredible resource for geographical, historical, cultural and even linguistic, phonetic and phonological information on communities and their dialects.

Putting it into historical context ——————————

- Accents change over time. Influences come and go and it is important to know the period of the play you are doing and how your character fits into the social mix of the time. The accents in much of London today bear little or no relation to the accents of 50 years ago. Today in the early days of the 21st century some young people of London have an accent heavily influenced by the sounds of African, Jamaican and Bengali, whereas the influences in the early 20th century were French, Irish and Jewish. New accents appear with the arrival of another wave of incomers: accents such as Arabic/Chicago or Bengali/Bradford. We can't always be totally historically accurate, but knowing where your accent comes from and even where it's going will enable you to make informed choices about what to do and how to do it.

- Where you can, find a sample speaker from the right period for the play/character you are doing. It may take a bit of searching through historical sound archives. A 50-year-old speaker recorded in 1920 is giving you a window into an accent that reaches back to the 1870s. It would be inappropriate to use the accent of a present-day 17-year-old for plays such as *The Bright and Bold Design* (1930s Stoke-on-Trent), *Men Should Weep* (1930s Glasgow) or *The Accrington Pals* (First World War Accrington).

2

THE FOUNDATIONS

IN THIS CHAPTER...

You will learn how to lay the **Foundations** of an accent. Solid foundations hold the whole structure of the accent in place.

When asked what makes one accent different from another, most people will point to differences in tune (what we will call the 'groove', page 149), two or three vowels (the 'shapes', page 113), and maybe one or two consonants (the 'bite', page 55). These are all valid, important observations, but underpinning all of these are the foundations on which the groove, shapes and bite sit.

One day we were sharing our stories of how we each discovered that we had a passion for sounds and accents. When Jan was young, she and her friend Julie Brown used to pretend they were French. This didn't involve any French language, just gobbledygook using a generally 'French' sound. They also pretended to be the 'Fonz' doing an American accent, and Liza Goddard in Skippy *doing an Australian accent. At the tender age of ten, Jan taught Julie what the difference was between those accents, explaining that:*

- *'American' was in the back of the mouth.*

- *'French' needed to have a particular tone to it.*

- *'Australian' was similar to 'London', but you needed to smile and grit your teeth.*

Contained within these apparently naïve early descriptions are the first three of the four building blocks that are the foundations of an accent.

To establish solid accent foundations, you will need these three elements to be firmly in place:

- **The Zone** – Where the sound is placed.

- **The Tone** – The resonant quality of the accent.

- **The Setting** – The setting of the muscles of the face and mouth.

With these in place, and because the voice is not a static building, you will need one more element…

- **The Direction** – The direction in which the voice is sent.

Without these foundations your accent will be unfocused and difficult to sustain, but with all four elements working together you create the solid foundations on which the rest of the accent is built.

So before we go any further let's learn how to:

- Focus the voice in a specific **Zone**.

- Hear and create a specific **Tone**.

- Feel and sustain a specific **Setting**.

- Send the voice in the right **Direction**.

…and thereby build your **Foundations**.

THE ZONE

Each accent has a resonant focal point, or 'placement', in the mouth that we call a **Zone**.

Small changes in the shaping of the throat and mouth, tongue and soft palate affect which zone the voice resonates in. These changes are very small, and the muscles do not respond easily to direct instructions. They are programmed as 'mimicry' muscles, and from an early age we all use them to learn how to recreate the sounds we hear around us. Be bold: dive into copying the sounds in this section and wake up your basic childhood skills of mimicry. Do this consciously and notice the results you get. This will increase your skill at zoning. Notice how the voice feels in the mouth and where you feel it is focused. In order to focus your voice into the specific zone for your accent, it helps to have a good visual image of the inside of your mouth and to picture the different zones you are aiming for.

As you can see in the illustration below there are seven zones.

These zones are focused on the following areas:

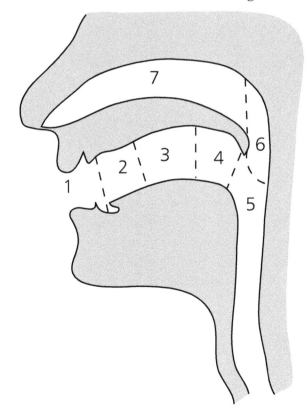

Zone 1: The **Teeth and Lips**

Zone 2: The **Gum-ridge**

Zone 3: The **Hard Palate**

Zone 4: The **Soft Palate** and **Uvula**

Zone 5: Down into the **Pharynx** (throat)

Zone 6: Up into the **Naso-pharynx** (behind the nose)

Zone 7: The **Nasal Cavity** (right inside and down the nose)

When you focus your voice into each of these zones, the quality of the sound will change.

- In order to isolate the effect of changing the zone, listen to the voice being focused into each of the seven zones.
- Then listen to Jan as she tunes in and finds different accents lurking in each zone.

Notice the way we 'tune in' to the zone and then keep the voice in that zone, counting on *one note*. By staying on one note you can hear that it is the *resonance* that changes from zone to zone, and not the actual pitch of the voice.

Listen to us a few times and then have a go yourself.

Pick a comfortable note of your own to use and stick to it. You can reverse the order if you find it easier. Sometimes the zones at the back of the mouth are easier to feel, as the vibrations are creating stronger sensations.

You may find it hard not to change accent: each zone may bring a different accent to your mouth. That's the power of zoning!

Visualise the zones inside your mouth as you speak with us. See your voice travelling and hitting a specific target point in each zone. Do this a few times to get a good sense of each zone. Remember you are flexing those mimicry muscles and using your mind's eye! The more you do it, the better you'll get.

Feel the vibrations hitting the target points in each zone.

7 **Nasal cavity:** Aim the voice right down the nose, and only the nose, and feel it vibrating.

6 **Naso-pharynx:** Aim the voice behind the soft palate, keep those vibrations at the back of the nose, not down it.

5 **Pharynx:** Aim the voice to the back of the mouth in the space behind the tongue. (You may need to think of a yawn to create more space.)

4 **Soft palate** and **Uvula:** Aim the voice onto the soft palate and uvula. Feel this soft tissue vibrating.

3 **Hard palate:** Aim the voice straight up into the roof of the mouth. Feel the vibrations driving up onto the hard palate and *through the bone*.

2 **Gum-ridge:** Aim the voice forward onto the gum-ridge. Feel the full effect of the vibrations in this area. Vibrations also pass through the gum-ridge and upper lip and vibrate in the nostrils.

1 **Teeth and lips:** Aim the voice onto the teeth and lips and into the open space beyond! This time you may not feel the vibrations very strongly as you are aiming right through and out of the mouth with the voice touching nothing else on the way.

Some of the zones may be easier for you to feel and hear than others. Keep working on seeing, hearing, and feeling them to really develop sensitivity and flexibility.

> **TOP TIP**
> As the voice moves in the mouth you may **think** it sounds higher at the front and lower at the back. Don't be tempted to change the **pitch**: let the zone do the work!

2

THE TONE

The second essential element in building the foundations of an accent is the ability to identify and *sustain* its specific **tone**.

Ever stop talking and think you can still hear the *sound* of your voice? Or maybe someone else stopped talking and you could still hear the sound of *their* voice? Listen to a person speak for a while, don't listen to the words, but just listen to the *tone* of their voice. You can hear a tonal drone that underpins the voice no matter where the music or pitch may travel. Think of the way bagpipes sound, with the constant drone underneath the complex melody: that's the kind of thing we mean.

Every accent has a tone of its own, and when you listen to all the examples on the downloadable tracks you can hear how different tones can be. Just as with the zone, the tone is created by small changes in the shaping of the throat and mouth, tongue and soft palate. The effect can be to give a sound greater depth or make it more lightweight; it may seem 'harsher' or 'softer'. Think of the twang of Tennessee or the soft airy sound of upper-class Georgia. Think about how the Queen sounds, or David Beckham. We might use words such as 'thin' or 'tight' to describe the Queen's sound. We might use words such as 'light' and 'sweet' to describe David Beckham's. We use words like this all the time to describe voices: brassy, throaty, nasal, plummy, hoarse, squeaky, boomy, whiney, etc… It is not the *pronunciation* of words we are describing here, but rather the *tone* of the voice, the quality of the sound – in fact the balance of the tonal frequencies.

- Listen to these speakers. Listen not to *what* they say, but only to the *tone* of their voices, the noise their voices make. (You can hear us in the background making this clearer!)
  Manchester   Cockney   Standard English
- Listen to the way we identify and tune in to the tone of each, and then sustain that tone as we count to ten.

Now get those mimicry muscles working. Have a go yourself. Match your tone to the *tonal quality* of the speakers.

Of course, the zone and the tone are intrinsically connected: you can't get one without the other! Identify which zone you feel the tone vibrating in. Feel the tone resonating in that zone.

Visualise the tone resonating in the specific zone you have identified.

Have a go with our other sample speakers (TRACKS 84-100) in this way in order to really exercise your zoning and toning skills. Don't try to be subtle. Really try to mimic what you hear. Be playful and have fun.

THE SETTING

By layering the tone and zone together you are creating anchors for the foundations of the accent in your mouth. In order to move through the zones and find new tones, you will have had to change the position or shape of your tongue, mouth, soft palate, lips and/or jaw. You were changing your **Setting**.

Take a look at the active articulators in 'Knowing your equipment' (page 202). They are the **cheeks**, the **lips**, the **jaw**, the **tongue** and the **soft palate**. These are the movable parts of your speech system, and all of these are involved in creating a **setting**. Your own articulators are held in their particular setting for your own accent and in order to do another accent they will have to find a new setting.

> *We were laughing as we wrote this section, because we remembered a game that we play when we're on the tube. We watch people in the next carriage and try to guess their accents simply by watching their faces as they speak. Even though we can't hear them, we are able to see some of the muscular settings of the face and mouth that contribute to the sound. Jan's mum, who is not famed for her ability to do accents or impressions, gets one bit spot on: when recreating a speaker she will always pull a slightly bizarre face! What she recognises is that the speaker is using a different muscular setting from her own. Fortunately (perhaps) she doesn't have to walk on stage and recreate an accent, so her work can stop there; but if she did, this would be a very useful starting point.*

In each accent the muscles of the face and mouth are shaped and held in a particular position. After all, if your mouth has to make the same set of moves over and over again it is bound to take up a position that makes those moves possible. In Arabic, for example, the root of the tongue is tense, ready to make those guttural sounds; in Indian the tongue tip is curled up and back for the retroflexed consonants; in Canadian the body of the tongue is bunched up, ready for those Rs; and so on…

*When we worked with an Australian actress (who did have to walk on stage), she said that in order to get into the English accent she had to relax her cheek muscles, get a 'scooped-out' feeling in the cheeks, and make a gap between her top and bottom back teeth. These three small adjustments made a huge difference to her **setting**, and through this setting she was more able to find and keep the zone and tone.*

Feel your muscles being held in different settings from the ones they're used to while you count to ten, or speak the days of the week. Focus on maintaining the setting, letting that inform the sound. We've gone through the articulators one at a time so that you can really focus on the effect changes in each of them can have.

Listen to the way the quality of the sound changes with each setting.

Look at the changes in the mirror.

Cheeks:
- Let the cheeks hang loose.
- Scoop the cheeks inwards.
- Widen the cheeks in a half smile.

Lips:
- Tighten the inner muscle of the lips ('cat's bottom'!).
- Stretch the lips out into a thin, wide line.
- Pout with fat lips.

Jaw:
- Clench the teeth.
- Bounce the jaw open for the vowels.
- Drop and hold the jaw loosely open.

Tongue:
- Squeeze the tongue up and forward in a strong 'EE' position.
- Relax the tongue and let it feel fat in the mouth.
- Hold the back of the tongue high up in the mouth, as if about to do a 'G'.

Soft Palate:
- Hold a yawn at the back of your mouth.
- Let the soft palate become heavy, squashing the space at the back of the mouth, like almost saying 'NG'.

Now listen to us as we describe the settings of three accents as we speak in them:

Yorkshire	Scottish	Cockney
Cheeks: Loose	**Cheeks:** Soft	**Cheeks:** Held
Lips: Slack	**Lips:** Pouted and held small	**Lips:** Flat (corners pinched)
Jaw: Dropped	**Jaw:** Mid-open	**Jaw:** Closed
Tongue: Heavy and flat	**Tongue:** Rolled forward and gripped	**Soft Palate:** Low
Soft Palate: High	**Soft Palate:** Low	

So how do you identify what the setting of a particular accent is? Well, it really is a circular process: get the tone and zone and you have the setting; get the setting and you have the tone and zone. If you can see a speaker then you will get some visual clues, and when you listen to a speaker your own muscles may well find the setting for you through a sort of sympathetic response; but if you're still not sure, the biggest clue is to be found in one of the smallest sounds the speaker makes…

The Hesitation sound

The hesitation sound 'um' or 'uh', that you hear when speakers are thinking of what to say next, is the sound that is made when the mouth relaxes into its own neutral setting.

By listening for and recreating this sound you can often identify the setting of an accent, especially if it is very different from your own!

Listen to all these hesitation sounds… You can hear how different they can be from one accent to another!

Copy the hesitation sounds and feel the shapes you have to make to get each sound right.

Freeze mid-sound and notice the position your muscles are in. This can give you the neutral setting for that accent.

Do the above exercise, and this time look in the mirror to see how your face changes from one accent to another.

Finding and keeping the setting is *crucial*. It enables you to sustain your accent and gives it authenticity. What is most significant, and often surprising to realise, is that the settings you have to hold to make these sounds are the relaxed *effortless* settings of those speakers. When they stop speaking it is those settings that their muscles fall back into.

> **TOP TIP**
> *Make sure you relax back into the setting of the **accent** between phrases of speech, and not your **own** setting. The accent is still there in the setting of your muscles, even when you are not speaking!*

THE DIRECTION

One more thing…

…by layering the **Zone**, **Tone** and **Setting** together you have established the essential foundations of an accent, but to make it come alive you need one more thing: a direction in which to send it. Not sure what we mean? When working on any accents think about the way in which the sound seems to travel out of the mouth: it may be quite different from your own accent. When you listen to different accents you can imagine seeing the sound travelling around and out of the mouth in different directions, like arrows. It could be travelling forwards, backwards or even sideways. Listen to these examples to hear what we mean.

- *Cockney*: Forward onto hard palate and teeth.

- *Liverpool*: Spilling sideways.

- *Manchester*: Held at the back, circling.

- *Newcastle*: Lurching back and forth.

- *Glasgow*: Falling back.

- *NSEA*: Forward and out like a wave.

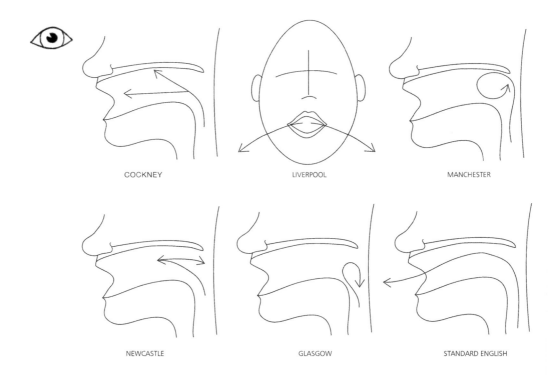

COCKNEY   LIVERPOOL   MANCHESTER

NEWCASTLE   GLASGOW   STANDARD ENGLISH

Using the KIT LIST or Set Text (pages 179–180), have a go at any of these accents and send your voice in the described direction and you will notice what an effect it has!

PUTTING IT ALL TOGETHER

Zone, Tone, Setting and **Direction**: these four elements each work hand in hand to give an accent solid foundations.

Below we have given brief descriptions of the foundations of six example accents.

As you listen to the six examples, use your new skills of seeing, feeling and hearing the zone, tone, setting and direction.

It is hard to describe a tonal quality on paper. It is the quality that *you hear* that counts. We have used words that describe the tones we hear and what those tones reminded us of. You may well think of other things…

	ZONE	TONE	SETTING AND HESITATION		DIRECTION
NSEA [TRACK 98]	2	Soft and Velvety.	Loose jaw. Slight lift in top lip. Soft palate high and bouncy. Tongue tip active, often flicking up to gum-ridge.	**'UHM'**	Forward out of the mouth like a wave, avoiding all obstacles on the way!
Cockney [TRACK 97]	3	Brass Band.	Jaw held. Lips flat and thin. Soft palate low.	**'AM'**	Punched up onto the hard palate and forward onto the teeth.
Liverpool [TRACK 94]	4	Foghorn.	Jaw held close. Cheeks and lips wide. Soft palate low. Tongue held high.	**'E..M'**	Spilling sideways.
Glasgow [TRACK 91]	5	The sound of effortful lifting!	Cheeks loose. Lips slightly lifted and pouting. Tongue rolled forward and squeezed into 'EE' position. Soft palate low.	**'EYM'**	Falling backwards.
Manchester [TRACK 93]	6	Trumpet with mute.	Back of tongue high. Soft palate low.	**'OEM'**	Held at the back and circling.
Newcastle [TRACK 92]	5 – 3	Owl hooting	Cheeks and lips move suddenly between shapes. Back on tongue tense and raised. Jaw held and bouncy.	**'EM'**	Lurching back and forth.

2

> **TOP TIP**
> *Remember, at this stage you are only listening for the **Zone, Tone, Setting** and **Direction**. You may well notice other things, but don't be distracted by all the other elements that make up an accent. These are just the foundations!*

You and the New: Foundations

YOU

Identify the elements of your own foundations:

- What **Zone** does your accent focus into?
- What does the **Tone** sound like?
- What does the muscular **Setting** feel like?
- In what **Direction** does the sound travel out of the mouth?

The Hesitation Sound

What is the hesitation or neutral sound you make?

Put your observations in the 'Foundations' section of the **You and the New Chart** on page 192. This way you will be able to see how any new accent compares to your own (photocopy this page, or download fresh copies at **www.howtodoaccents.com**).

THE NEW: the Foundations Checklist

When you are working on a specific accent use this checklist every time to build your solid foundations:

- What **Zone** does it focus into?
- What does the **Tone** sound like?
- What does the **Setting** feel like?
- In what **Direction** does the sound travel out of the mouth?

The Hesitation Sound

What is the hesitation or neutral sound your new accent makes?

Listen to Tracks 1 – 3 to hear the Zone, Tone and Settings being explored.

Listen to Track 4 to hear different hesitation sounds.

3

THE TWO PLANETS

(Rhotic vs. Non-Rhotic)

IN THIS CHAPTER...

You will learn all about **rhoticity** (and no, that isn't a way of cooking a chicken). When it comes to accents the world divides into two planets:

- **Rhotic** – People who *always* say an R *whenever* it is written – ORDER MOTHER CART HERE

- **Non-rhotic** – People who *only* say an R if there is a vowel sound *spoken* after it – HARRY HERO BRING SACRED RIGHT

More significantly you'll discover which planet *you* are on, and how to pass as a local on the other!

There was a time when English was all on one planet: Planet Rhotic. That's why the Rs are there in the written word. But over time the world divided in two…

On Planet Rhotic life is simple: every R that they see, they say! ('Of course we do!' the Rhotics cry.)

On Planet Non-Rhotic, however, life is a bit more complicated. Here speakers only pronounce an R if it is directly followed by a spoken vowel sound. So they pronounce the R in *run, horrid, flowery,* but not in *heart, far* or *flower.* What was historically a vowel plus R will often be said as a **long vowel**, making **HEART** become **HAAHT**, and **CAR** become **CAH**.

So who's on which planet? Well, on Planet Rhotic you have most of **America**, **Barbados**, **Canada**, **India**, **Ireland** and **Scotland**, the English **West Country**, and parts of **Lancashire**.

On Planet Non-Rhotic you will find **Africa**, **Australia**, most of the **Caribbean**, most of **England**, most of **New Zealand** and **Wales**, many North East coast American accents, such as **New York City** and **Boston** as well as some older accents of the deep south of America, and many **African American** accents. **Singapore** and **Malaysia** are also two examples of countries in Asia with a non-rhotic accent, while in Canada non-rhotic accents have been reported in south-western **New Brunswick**, various isolated parts of **Newfoundland**, and **Lunenburg County, Nova Scotia**.

This can lead to confusion as we move from planet to planet, as Edda found when giving her surname to register at a Canadian hotel. She pronounced 'SHARPE' the English way, 'SHAHP'. Looking down she saw the receptionist write the word, 'SHOP'!

THE TWO PLANETS

The two planets are divided by two very different rules regarding the use of R. They are labelled either RHOTIC or NON-RHOTIC.

On Planet **Rhotic**:

They *always* say an R whenever it is written, and *never* say one if it is not written.

On Planet **Non-Rhotic**:

They *only* say an R if it is followed by a vowel sound, and *may* say one when it is not even written.

When it comes to doing *any* accent it is important to know the answers to the following questions:

- **Which planet are YOU on?**
- **Which planet is your NEW accent on?**
- **Are they the SAME planet?**
- **Are you on DIFFERENT planets?**

Which planet are YOU on?

Look at this phrase: **Law and Order.**

● How many Rs do you see?

Now speak the phrase in your own accent, flowing from word to word.

● How many Rs do you *say?*

Some of you will be saying two Rs, both in the word **Order.** But others of you may only be saying one R, and you'll be saying it where there isn't even one written, like this: **law r-and.** What's more, you probably don't even realise you're doing it! That's what we mean by two planets.

Still not sure which planet you're on? Say the *name* of this letter the way you normally would when reciting the alphabet: **R.**

Do you *feel* your tongue move to shape an R? Then your accent is on Planet Rhotic!

Does your tongue stay flat, making more of an 'AH'? Then your accent is on Planet Non-Rhotic!

Which planet is your NEW accent on?

Have a listen to track 5. You will hear three rhotic speakers. Notice the R is spoken whenever it appears in a word. Is this what your new accent does?

MaRgaRet caught heR daughteR pouRing wateR oveR the floweRs.

Now listen to track 6. You will hear three non-rhotic speakers. Notice the way they all drop the R that is clearly written in the word because the next sound is not a vowel. Is this what your new accent does?

Park Stern Here Poor Hair Court

Is it the SAME planet as you?

If you and your new accent are on the same planet, life is a *lot* easier. Have a quick read of the section that applies to you both, just to confirm what happens on your planet. Knowing your own funny quirks can help you understand why a new accent may be going awry

Are you on DIFFERENT PLANETS?

NON-RHOTIC becoming RHOTIC?

If your own accent follows a non-rhotic pattern, but your new accent is rhotic, look carefully at 'Spotlight on Planet Rhotic' (pg 43) to learn the rather sensible ways of those rhotic folk.

RHOTIC becoming NON-RHOTIC?

If your own accent follows a rhotic pattern, but your new accent is non-rhotic, look carefully at 'Spotlight on Planet Non-Rhotic' (pg 47) to learn the rather curious ways of those non-rhotic folk.

SPOTLIGHT ON PLANET RHOTIC

The first rule on Planet Rhotic is:

● If you see an R you say it…and if you don't, *don't*!

That sounds straightforward, but here are two big mistakes that non-rhotic speakers make when doing rhotic accents that *always* give them away:

● Leaving out Rs that should be there.

● Adding ones that shouldn't be there.

And believe us, non-rhotics will often do this without even realising.

So here's how to avoid those two killer mistakes.

How to put in Rs that *should* be there

The way that words are written reflects the rhotic view of the world (and it certainly confirms that once upon a time *all* English speakers were rhotic). Basically, if there is an R in the spelling of a word, a rhotic speaker will *always* say it.

Look at this sentence. We have highlighted all the Rs in it. To be rhotic you will need to say all these Rs!

MaRgaRet caught heR daughteR pouRing wateR oveR the floweRs.

● Listen to our three rhotic speakers saying this sentence and hear how all the Rs are spoken.
   ● *Scottish*
   ● *Standard American*
   ● *Northern Irish*

Notice that although the *way* they say the R is different (in this case Tap, Molar, Retroflex – more about these terms when we discuss 'R' in The Bite, page 57), *when* they say it is the same. That's Planet Rhotic.

● Choose an R that feels familiar and comfortable to do. Remember, for the purpose of this exercise it doesn't matter which kind of R you use, so long as you are aware of *when* you are saying it! If you want to be more specific you will of course need to learn the right *kind* of R for the accent you are doing… (More about that on pages 57–65).

● Speak the sentence yourself, saying all the Rs in the same places as the rhotic speakers. That simply means wherever one is written.

> **TOP TIP**
> ● *Words with an R will now take a little longer to say because there is an extra movement for your tongue to make. So slow down!*
> **SATURDAY**
> ● *Your tongue isn't familiar with the new movement, especially when it has to happen quickly. Practise the move to make it fluent and easy.*
> **CORNER**

How *not* to add Rs that *shouldn't* be there!

One of the biggest mistakes non-rhotic people make when doing a rhotic accent (such as Standard American) is to *add* Rs where they *shouldn't*. If you're an American you'll know how baffling and annoying that is, and many of us non-rhotics don't even know we've done it!

When doing an American accent you may be quite happy to buy a 'pizzar in Americar', but of course, you would be wrong. So why do we do it? Well, in non-rhotic accents, the dropped R means that many words rhyme that wouldn't if we kept the R. Look at these pairs of words and you'll see what we mean:

Court Caught   Pour Paw   Sore Saw   Sort Sought

In a **non-rhotic** accent the two words in these pairs sound the same. Here lies the root of the problem. Once a non-rhotic successfully learns to put the R in the first word, they will automatically want to put one in the second, thus keeping the same sound… Mistake! This is your non-rhotic sound pattern at work, and *not* the pattern of your new accent. In a rhotic accent these words sound completely different. A non-rhotic may think it sounds fine, but to a rhotic ear it will sound at best confusing and at worst comical.

Now look at these two lists: same problem, different sound!

Actor   Brother   Wilbur   Author
Linda   Pizza   America   Plaza

Again, in non-rhotic accents these words all end with the same small UH sound (called the **schwa** – see page 124), and once you have learned to put an R on the end of the first set you may find yourself putting Rs on the second set too! But in rhotic accents they are *completely different*! This may seem obvious, but try it and you will see how hard it can sometimes be.

- Say **Court**, pronouncing the R.
- Say **Caught**, without an R.
- Say the two words one after the other, ensuring that one has an R and one doesn't.

Do this a few times to get used to this new pattern. Break the rhyme!

Now put them in this sentence: **I caught the bus to go to court.**

Now try these:
- Say **Wilbur**, pronouncing the final R.
- Say **Linda**, without adding a final R!
- Say them a few times feeling the different ending.

And now put it all together in this sentence: **Linda caught Wilbur in court.**

And just when you thought you'd cracked it…

You will also need to learn the rhotic way of gliding from one vowel to another across two words *without* inserting an R!

Say these phrases and notice if you have even a slight urge to put an R between the words where we've marked them. Maybe you don't notice yourself do it. Get another non-rhotic person to say them and listen to what they do.

Linda and I	**Law and Justice**
Linda Rand I	**Law Rand Justice**

A rhotic speaker would simply *never* do this! Not only do they not do this, they find it extremely noticeable and baffling when they hear other people do it.

Here's what to do:

- Glide from one word to the other, maintaining the open shape at the end of one word and the beginning of the other, keeping the tip of the tongue relaxed behind the bottom teeth.
- It can really help to think of the second word as part of the first:

  Lindaand I   **Lawnd Justice**

This is what the rhotics do!

To do any rhotic accent it is *vital* to practise these glides, as *all* rhotic accents use them.

Practise your new R patterns on this sentence. Remember to put in Rs that should be there and not to put in Rs that shouldn't!

Wilbur told his daughter (not DOOR-ter!) **Linda** (not lindER!) **to talk about law and** (not LORand!) **justice, but it bored her. He had an awesome** (not OARsome!) **idea** (not ideaR!)

This is the pattern that you need to be rhotic, look out for Rs like a hork – oops, we mean *hawk*. Don't let that non-rhotic rhyme pattern lead you into mistakes. After all, it's important to distinguish 'the dog's paw' from 'the dog's pore'…

SPOTLIGHT ON PLANET NON-RHOTIC

Okay, rhotic folk! Gone are the simple days when an R was simply said wherever it appeared in a word.

> On Planet Non-Rhotic you can think of the R in two ways:
> - *Only ever* say an R if it is *followed* by a vowel sound.
> - *Never* say an R if it is *followed* by a consonant.

- Look at this word: **Cargo**
  Although there's an R written, it's followed by a consonant, so *don't say* it!
- And this word: **Order**
  There are two Rs written here; the first R is followed by a consonant (D) and the second R ends the word, so *don't say* them!
- Now look at this word: **Hero**
  This R is followed by a vowel sound, so *do say* it!
- And what about this word? **Hairy**
  Although the Y looks like a consonant it is spoken here as a vowel sound, so…this R is followed by a vowel so *do say* it!
- And what about these teasers? **Here Care**
  It may look like the R is followed by a vowel, but it isn't a *spoken vowel* so bang goes the R: *don't say* it!

How to lose those Rs

Listen to these non-rhotic speakers saying the following words without pronouncing the Rs.

- *Norfolk, Wales, Newcastle:*

  Park   Stern   Here   Poor   Hair   Court

- Say the words yourself, losing the Rs *completely*.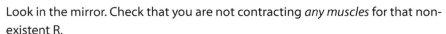
- Instead of the R, just lengthen the vowel.
- Keep the tip of your tongue behind your bottom teeth.

Look in the mirror. Check that you are not contracting *any muscles* for that non-existent R.

Be careful: your tongue may *think* it's not doing an R, and maybe it doesn't sound like an R to you, but is your tongue still moving? Even a little bit? Even

---

the *slightest* movement of the tongue, however small, will still be heard as an R by a non-rhotic speaker. It really does need to be dropped *completely*!

> **TOP TIP**
> *We have found that it can really help rhotic people to re-write the words without an R in the spelling, and to see the words this way:*
> **Mahgret pawed the watuh   Richud loved flowuh powuh**

 Now practise on this little paragraph. Remember the rule: if it's followed by a vowel *sound* you say it; if it's not you don't! (**r** = say; r = don't say)

Margaret, Rhys and Richard poured water all over the flowers, they loved pouring water.

So that's how to lose those Rs… Now for when to put them back in!

Doing the R bounce

Because a non-rhotic R is only said when followed by a vowel it is no longer just a letter in a word, it now has a special job to do: it's a springboard off which the vowel can jump, giving a bounce to the start of syllables! This results in these three great features of non-rhotic accents:

● The **mid-word bounce** (see below): **Gerry = Ge-rry**

● The **linking bounce** (page 49): **Car alarm = Ca-ralarm**

● The **intrusive bounce** (page 50): **Linda and I = Linda-rand I**

The mid-word bounce

Look at these words with Rs in the middle:

Very   Sorry   Harry   Worry   Spirit   Courage

For many people on Planet Rhotic the R is part of the first syllable and the two syllables glide into one another:

Ver–y   Sorr–y   Harr–y   Worr–y   Spir–it   Cour–age

But on Planet Non-Rhotic the R is used to bounce into the second syllable. The syllables are clearly separated. The vowel before the R must be kept absolutely clean of any influence from the R that follows it!

 Ve – ry   So – rry   Ha – rry   Wo – rry   Spi – rit   Cou – rage

● *American:* rhotic

● *Neutral Standard English:* non-rhotic

Speak the example words yourself slowly and carefully, feeling the separation of the syllables, keeping the R clear of the preceding vowel and using the R to bounce into the following syllable.

Ve – ry   So – rry   Ha – rry   Wo – rry   Spi – rit   Cou – rage

The linking bounce

As we have seen, when an R *ends* a word a non-rhotic speaker won't say it because it's not followed by a spoken vowel:

Car   More   Here

However, if the next word *starts with a vowel*…then the R has its job back! The non-rhotic speaker 'links' the two words with the R. It is important to note that this R does not *end* the first word, but bounces into the second:

Car Ralarm   More Rover   Here RI am

Listen to these speakers from *Norfolk, Liverpool* and *Newcastle* dropping the R when the word is on its own, but using it to link to the next word!
- **Car   Car Ralarm**
- **More   More Rover**
- **Here   Here RI am**

● First say the word on its own without the R.
● Now put the words together using the R to start the following word *without breaking the flow.*

And try this phrase with the linking bounces marked:

John tipped water rinto the plants, more rover Wilbur rand Linda didn't!

> **TOP TIP**
> *Watch out! This **won't** happen if the speaker breaks the flow or breathes between the words!*
> *Dropping the R often makes rhotic speakers feel so good in their new non-rhotic accent that they do it too much, missing the authenticity that the linking bounce can give.*

And here's the final and somewhat cheeky little bounce…

The intrusive bounce

On Planet Non-Rhotic, just because there's no R written, it doesn't mean you can't do one.

Some non-rhotics just *hate* having two vowel sounds next to each other. They feel they just *have* to insert a consonant to help with the flow!

For some non-rhotic speakers, it can feel entirely natural to insert an R to make a cheeky little bounce from one vowel to another!

Edda and Jan = 'Edda Rand Jan'.

This is often referred to as an Intrusive R, because the *sound* of an R intrudes where there is no *written* R. (Cheeky!)

It is most often used to bounce between two words:

India Rand China   Draw Rout   Linda Ris

And it can even happen *within* a word…

PawRing   DrawRing

…which can make the words **Pouring** and **Pawing** sound exactly the same!

● *Norfolk, West Midlands, Yorkshire:*

Linda Ris drawRing India Rand China

However odd it sounds to you, it is so natural to many non-rhotic speakers that they don't even know they are doing it!

● Have a go yourself inserting a gentle R to bounce from one vowel to the other.

Here are some more phrases to play with:

● **I saw a boy** becomes **I saw Ra boy**

● **I had an idea about that** becomes **I had an idea Rabout that**

● **Linda and I sat in the drawing room** becomes
Linda Rand I sat in the drawRing room

Yes, people really do this! It is a very common feature of non-rhotic accents such as London, Liverpool and New York.

It is not a feature of *all* non-rhotic accents, however. Some accents of the deep south of America don't do it and the 'posher' speakers of Standard English frown on it!

When it comes to rhoticity, getting it right or wrong can really make or break your accent. There are some accents that are 'hybrids'. This happens when one accent becomes influenced by another from the other planet. The American South is losing many of its non-rhotic accents, for example, while Dublin and much of the South West of England are losing their rhoticity. Sometimes the dominant patterns of the country begin to take over the smaller accent pockets; sometimes social aspiration or association means that an accent will change. When you hear a hybrid, be extra careful to notice which Rs are kept and which are lost. This is why it is so important to know the background of any accent you wish to learn.

3

You and the New: The Two Planets

YOU

- Which planet are YOU on?
  Is your own accent rhotic or non-rhotic?
  If you are non-rhotic, do you use a linking bounce or an intrusive bounce?

Go to the 'You and the New' chart on page 193 and make a note of your patterns in The Two Planets section so that you can compare any new accent to your own (photocopy this page or download fresh copies at **www.howtodoaccents.com**).

THE NEW: The Two Planets Checklist:

When you are working on a specific accent use this checklist every time to be sure you are on the right planet:

- Which planet is your NEW accent on?
  RHOTIC
  (*always* say an R whenever it is written)
  NON-RHOTIC
  (*only* say an R when followed by a vowel, and *sometimes* say one when it isn't even written)

- Are you on the SAME planet?
  Both Rhotic: Check *what kind* of R they use (see 'Major Players: R' on page 57)
  Both Non-Rhotic: Check *what kind* of R they use and when (see Major Players on page 57) and check whether you both use linking or intrusive Rs or not!

- Are you on DIFFERENT planet?
  Remember, if your new accent is on the opposite planet from yours, you will need to be extra vigilant. It will be vital to **learn the patterns** of the new accent and also **check what kind** of R they use and **when** (see 'Major Players: R' on page 57).

Listen to Track 5 to hear the RHOTIC planet in action.

Listen to Tracks 6–9 to hear the NON-RHOTIC planet in action.

RHOTICITY MAPS

UK and Ireland

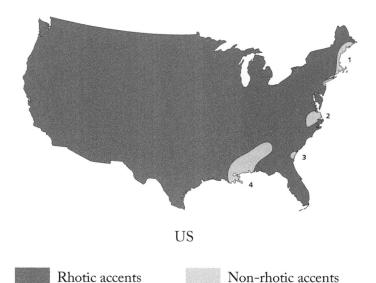

US

■ Rhotic accents   ■ Non-rhotic accents

UK and Ireland: Ireland and Scotland are wholly rhotic; England and Wales are non-rhotic, except for the South West and much of the Welsh-English border (1); areas of Pembrokeshire (2); and Central Lancashire (3).

US: This is more complex. Non-rhotic accents can traditionally be found in: the North East coast (including New York City and Boston) (1); areas of Virginia and North Carolina (2); parts of Georgia (including Savannah) (3); parts of Alabama, Mississippi and Louisiana (including New Orleans) (4). Non-rhoticity is more widespread within African-American accents.

4

THE BITE

(Consonants)

IN THIS CHAPTER...

You will discover the impact that consonants can have on an accent and the significant ways in which consonants differ from region to region.

We have identified the five **Major Players**: a set of consonants with the power to make or break your accent. Get these wrong and you risk your whole accent going down the pan! You cannot ignore the fact that Belfast uses a strong R, for example; the R must be said and said strongly. Ignore this fact and bang goes your Belfast.

The five Major Players are:

- **R** – tapping, bending, curling or bunching?
- **L** – light, dark, or not at all?
- **H** – to drop or not to drop?
- **NG** – are you running, runnin' runn'n or runningk for the bus?
- **TH** – are you with it, wivvit, widdit or wizzit?

Each of these Major Players is governed by patterns, 'rules' that determine both *how* to say them and also *when* to say them. The L alone can take you from one region to another if you don't get it right, as this little anecdote demonstrates…

Edda was asked to solve a problem for an actor whose own accent was strongly Lancashire. He was playing a character from the South Wales Valleys. Now, Lancashire is renowned for its heavy, dark L and the Welsh Valleys for its delicate light L. He found the vowels of the valleys particularly seductive and had great fun using them, but he had completely overlooked the consonants. Consequently he was speaking his new accent with South Welsh vowels and Lancashire consonants. The curious result had been that a Welsh woman in the audience complemented him on his North Wales accent! It was a seemingly small error, but it was enough to move him a hundred miles north.

We have also identified the **Major Issues** that can affect the sound and quality of all consonants. You will not only discover the powerful impact they can have on the overall quality of an accent, but you will also begin to develop the muscular flexibility to make those all-important changes.

We take a look at a cheeky set of consonants we call the **Springing Consonants**. These are 'consonants in vowels' clothing' and can pop up where you least expect them!

And finally there's a little detail we call **YOO**…

THE MAJOR PLAYERS

So here they are, introducing those five make-or-break sounds…

R – tapping, bending, curling or bunching?

L – light, dark, or not at all?

H – to drop or not to drop?

NG – are you running, runnin' runn'n or runningk for the bus?

TH – are you with it, wivvit, widdit or wizzit?

Get these wrong and you risk your whole accent going down the pan!

It's time to shine the spotlight on…

R L H NG TH

Tapping, bunching, curling, bending or substitute? ——

What makes R a Major Player is…

There are just so many different ways to make an R. To do an authentic accent you need to know *which type* of R an accent uses, when it uses it and how to do it.

Did you know different types of Rs have names? How about doing a 'retroflex R', a 'tap' or 'trill'? Or maybe you'd prefer to get your teeth round a 'molar R'?

How the R is made, the speed at which it moves, the zone it sits in and whether or not it touches the roof of the mouth: these will all have a dramatic effect, not just on the pronunciation of the word, but on the overall quality of the accent.

Taps ——

A tapped R is made when the tongue makes rapid contact with the roof of the mouth. It can be voiced or voiceless (see 'Voice: Feeling the buzz', page 89). If your tongue taps more than once in succession then you have made a trill! Taps are found in many English accents like Liverpool and the North of England, as well as Welsh and Scottish accents: these all use tapped Rs to a greater or lesser extent. Trills, on the other hand, tend to be more prevalent in accents rooted in languages other than English. Accents of English which use a trill will often use a simple tap when speaking rapidly or casually, and save a trill for more careful or emphatic speech. This is true of some African, Welsh and Scottish accents, for example.

How to do a gum-ridge tap

In a gum-ridge tap the tongue-tip lifts up and 'taps' the gum-ridge. It's a little like doing a quick, light D.

This is the sound of a gum-ridge tap:
- *Liverpool:* **Margaret and Gerry were very rowdy after drinking the terrible water.**

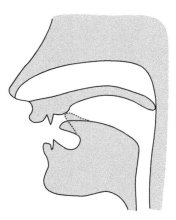

 If your tongue doesn't know what to do to make a gum-ridge tap, take it through the following steps:
- Lift the tip of your tongue up to your gum-ridge and tap it there lightly. This is the target in the mouth that the tongue needs to aim for.
- Whisper a long 'AAHH', breath only, and while breathing out make the gentlest tap you can, without breaking the flow of air. It will sound a little like: 'AHHDAHH'.
- Now, aim the tip of your tongue to your gum-ridge in these words, as if about to do a very light, gentle D, and let the tip make a quick flick against the ridge. Whisper the words first to focus on the feeling and the movement, and then use full voice. Use the tip of the tongue to flick into the next syllable.

Gerry   Very   Drinking   Terrible

How to do a retroflex tap

If you curl the tip of the tongue a little further back and tap behind the gum-ridge you have a 'retroflex tap'! This is the R heard in most accents derived from the Indian subcontinent.

● *Punjabi:* **Margaret and Gerry were very rowdy after drinking the terrible water.**

Tapped Rs can be found in both rhotic and non-rhotic accents, so make sure you try both patterns.

When an accent chooses to use a tapped R will often depend on the other sounds that surround it.

How to do a uvular tap

Although this is an unusual sound for English speakers, some older speakers from the North East of England and North Wales do use this sound in their accents. It is also quite common in other languages, such as French, German and Dutch.

For a uvular R the *back* of the tongue arches up and bounces off the soft palate.

This is the sound of a uvular R:

● *Old Newcastle:* **Margaret and Gerry were very rowdy after drinking the terrible water.**

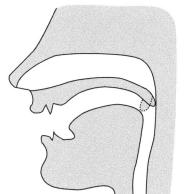

● Hold your tongue *almost* in a G position.
● Keep your *throat relaxed*.
● Say 'AH'.
● Gently bounce the softest G you can make off the soft palate.

Have a go using a uvular R on this practice sentence:

Margaret and Gerry were very rowdy after drinking the terrible water.

Your tongue may learn this quickly, but some tongues find it tricky. Work on the movement and sound in isolation.

Don't let it fall back into the throat, but keep it in the springy part of the tongue and soft palate. Be patient!

When this sound is repeated in quick succession you have a uvular trill. This is the sound of a purr, or Eartha Kitt!

> **TOP TIP**
> *Always check the specifics of **when** to tap. Some non-rhotic accents only tap between vowels, for example, and most accents don't tap Rs that **start** words.*

Bunches, curls and bends

The important thing with bunches, curls and bends is which *part* of your tongue does the bending, curling or bunching and which *zone* you resonate the sound in. Listen to accents of South West England, North America and Ireland and you'll hear all sorts of bending, curling and bunching Rs.

Bunched molar Rs are found far back in the mouth, retroflex Rs curl up towards the roof of the mouth, while a slight bend by the gum-ridge makes a free R. If it's not the tongue that bends at all, but the bottom lip instead, you have a little sound called an R substitute.

Let's begin at the back of the mouth with the bunched-up molar R.

How to do bunched molar Rs

The molar R is a strong feature of many North American accents, and it is often where English actors come unstuck.

The tongue body is retracted and lifted, the *sides* of the tongue press up and out against the top molars and the tip bunches back, disappearing into the body of the tongue.

This is the sound of a molar R:

● *American:* **Margaret and Gerry were very rowdy after drinking the terrible water.**

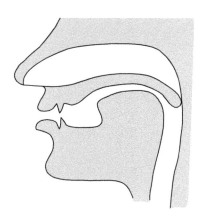

- Pull your tongue back and lift it up to scrape the sides along your top molars. Feel how the tongue bunches up.

- Look in the mirror as you do this and see how the tongue is pressed up in the mouth, while the tip disappears into the body of the tongue, which is drawn back in the mouth.

- Holding the tongue in that position, make the sound 'HRRR'.

That's a molar R. It is a very muscular action for the tongue to do, and if your tongue is not used to it, it may take a while to develop the agility to make this movement quickly. Try it on this sentence:

Margaret and Gerry were very rowdy after drinking the terrible water.

Did you know it is possible to focus your molar R into the different **zones** in your mouth? North Americans are especially sensitive to to the type of R they are hearing. Each region of America has its own special R resonance. Being able to move your molar R into different zones will enable you to move your accent from region to region across North America, giving you a fantastic key to accessing and anchoring the difference between Newfoundland and Ontario, Texas and California.

- Push the tongue up against the molars and slide it back and forth.
- Add voice to this slide and focus your sound into different zones.
- Hear how the resonance changes as you do this.
- Isolate different spots to stop off at in zones 2, 3 and 4 and listen to each of them in turn.

How to do curled retroflex Rs

The roof of the mouth is home to the retroflex R. It can be heard in Northern Ireland and accents of the West of England and Central Lancashire. It may be fully retroflex, or it may be bunching back with just a little curl of the tip. To do a full retroflex R, the tongue tip curls right up and back in the mouth; the jaw is held a little open and the lips tend to round. (*Retro* = 'back'; *flex* = 'curl'.)

Retroflex Rs tend to resonate quite strongly. The focus of that resonance can be anywhere from the middle to the back of the mouth, in zones 3, 4, 5, or 6, depending on the degree of curling and retraction of the tongue. They can be made with or without 'nasal spill'! (See page 142.)

This is the sound of a retroflex R:

- *Northern Irish:* **Margaret and Gerry were very rowdy after drinking the terrible water.**

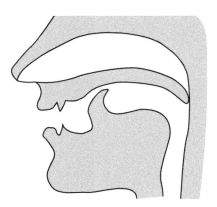

- Curl the tongue tip back and growl strongly.
- Focus the resonance in different zones in the mouth – 3, 4, 5 and 6 – as you curl back the tongue.
- Now use a retroflex R on the sentence:

  Margaret and Gerry were very rowdy after drinking the terrible water.

This is also a very muscular action for the tongue to perform, and if it's not used to it, it may take a while to develop the agility to make this movement quickly.

How to do bending free Rs

Moving to the front of the mouth we find the free R. This is the R used in many *Southern* (but not Northern) Irish accents and most English accents. Although the whole *body* of the tongue does not retract, bunch or curl, the *tip* is doing a lot of work. The tip curls or bends up towards the gum-ridge, without actually touching it. The cheeks may pull in to 'support' the tongue. The sound resonates in the mouth, neither on the back of the tongue nor spilling down the nose.

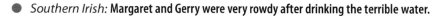

This is the sound of a free R.

● *Southern Irish:* **Margaret and Gerry were very rowdy after drinking the terrible water.**

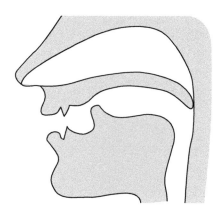

● Curl the tip of your tongue up towards your gum-ridge, without actually touching it.
● Keep it curling up and add your voice to this shape.
● Focus the sound onto the gum-ridge.
● The cheeks may pull in to support the shape.

Now use this free R in the sentence:

Margaret and Gerry were very rowdy after drinking the terrible water.

Getting this free R will be *especially* important for Northern Irish and North Americans if they want to travel to England and Southern Ireland.

> **TOP TIP**
> *If your own R is a substitute (see below) this will feel like work, but if your own R is a strong molar or retroflex this may not feel like an R at all!*

Substitutes

We have been moving the R from the back of the mouth to the front, starting with the molar, through the retroflex R and forward to the free R. Any further forward and the R will fall out of the mouth and land on the teeth and lips – and that is just what happens with the R substitute! It is effectively outside the mouth, it doesn't resonate in *any* of the zones.

How to do R Substitute

You may be familiar with the terms 'weak R', or a 'rabbity R'. There's a great example of one in the film *The Life of Brian*, when Michael Palin's Pontius Pilate calls to the crowd: 'Welease Woger!'. That is what we mean by an R substitute! In an R substitute the tongue doesn't move at all: instead, it hands the job of making the R over to the lips and teeth to form a kind of V or W. Some *individuals* have such a 'weak' R that their R substitute is indistinguishable from a W! Good examples of accents that use substitutes are New York City and the East End of London.

This is the sound of an R substitute:

● *London:* **Margaret and Gerry were very rowdy after drinking the terrible water.**

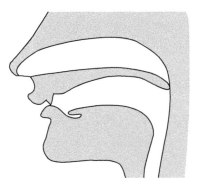

● Relax the tongue *completely*!
● Lift the inside of your bottom lip towards your top front teeth.
● Focus the sound onto the bottom lip.

Use this R substitute in the sentence:

Margaret and Gerry were very rowdy after drinking the terrible water.

Try the sentence as a Cockney, or imagine you are from New York City and you'll hear what a difference this sound can make.

You and the New: the R Checklist

This sentence will quickly illustrate what kind of R is used and when by you and/or your speaker:

R: Margaret, Linda and Gerry asked Peter if Roland started with 'R'.

YOU

- What kind of R do you use: do you tap, bunch, curl or bend, or has your R been substituted with a soft W?
- If you use a bunch or curl, what zone does the R resonate in?
- Do you always the same R or does it depend on the sounds around it?

Put your observations in the Major Player R section of the **You and the New Chart** on page 193 (photocopy this page or download fresh copies from **www.howtodoaccents.com**)

THE NEW

When you are working on a new accent, listen for this Major Player and use this checklist:

The R Checklist

Is the accent rhotic or non-rhotic (see checklist on page 52)?

How is the R made: does it tap, bunch, curl or bend, or has it been substituted with a soft W? And is it always the same R or does it depend on the sounds around it?

- **TAP:** What part of the tongue touches which part of the roof of the mouth?
- **BUNCH:** Which zone does it resonate in?
- **CURL:** Where does it curl to, which zone does it resonate in?
- **BEND:** Keep it nice and light at the front of the tongue.
- **SUBSTITUTE:** Bring the focus right onto the teeth and lips.

Whichever type of R and whichever pattern you use in your own accent, the chances are that other accents use a *different* one. Practise the new R and the new pattern so that this Major Player doesn't *break* your accent, but helps to *make* it instead.

Listen to Tracks 10–16 to hear the different types of R.

4

R **L** H NG TH

If ever there was a **Major Player** this is it! This seemingly innocent little sound is capable of transporting your accent from one place to another all on its own!

What makes L a Major Player is…

● **There are in fact three types of L: Light, Dark and W Substitute.**

● **There are *four* L patterns: accents that use…**

  1 **Only light L**

  2 **Only dark L**

  3 **Light and dark L combination**

  4 **Light L or dark L, plus W substitute combination**

Listen to the following accent examples, each using a different L pattern. Listen especially to the quality of the Ls in each example:

Larry the lazy lamb slept peacefully in the field until hailstones fell.

● Only light L: *Welsh*

Light L uses only the front of the tongue, and it feels and sounds light and delicate.

● Only dark L: *Manchester*

Dark L, on the other hand, uses the front *and back* of the tongue and feels and sounds heavy and muscular.

● Light and dark L combination: *Neutral Standard English*

These accents use a combination of the above two Ls:

● Light L and W substitute: *London*

Dark L and W substitute: *American Deep South*

These accents use a combination of Ls, but W substitute replaces the dark L before a consonant or at the end of a word. For W substitute the front of the tongue is *not used at all*, the back of the tongue raises and the lips round, making a W-like sound.

To do any accent you will need to know *how* to do each of the different Ls and *when* to use them! Remember, they can make or break your accent.

So here's how to do them…

How to do a Light L

Listen to us say the sentence using only light Ls and have a go yourself.

Larry the lazy lamb slept peacefully in the field until hailstones fell.

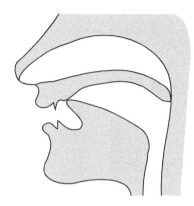

The essential quality of a light L is that *only the front of the tongue* is used to make it.

The 'lightness' is variable from 'quite light' to 'extremely light'. This will depend on how much of the front of the tongue makes contact: the less tongue used, the lighter the sound!

Look in the mirror...

- Stick your tongue out and point it up to the middle of your top lip.
- See the way the tongue narrows, points and curls up.
- Keeping the shape, draw the tongue into the mouth and place the pointy tip onto the gum-ridge.
- Hold this shape.

- Feel the open space at the back of your mouth and the tensing of the front of the tongue.
- Breathe out through this shape, thinking the vowel EE.
- Add your voice to this shape and you have a light L!
- Practise getting your tongue to and from this position:
  Leeleeleelee loolooloolooloo laalaalaalaa (etc).

- Listen to the quality of the sound you are making.

- Listen to us again…does your L sound the same?

So that's a light L. Many accents use *only* a light L: those of the Indian Sub-continent, most of Wales, all of Ireland and the far North East of England are all light L only accents. If your own accent doesn't use a light L your tongue will be learning a whole new shape. Keep practising the muscularity and sound until your tongue is confident forming it.

4

How to do a Dark L

 Listen to us doing the sentence using dark Ls and have a go yourself.

Larry the lazy lamb slept peacefully in the field until hailstones fell.

 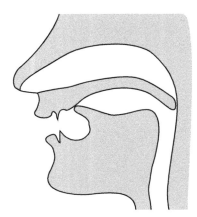 The essential quality of a dark L is that as well as the tongue tip touching the gum-ridge, the *back of the tongue is raised towards the soft palate.*

The 'darkness' is variable, from 'quite dark' to 'extremely dark'. This will depend on just how much of the back of the tongue rises. It is this added muscularity that can make the dark L tricky, especially if you are not used to it.

- Place your tongue tip on your gum-ridge and 'glue' it there.
- Hold the position and go to say an 'OO' sound…the back of the tongue raises towards a G position. This is the essential feature of a dark L.
- Hold all the internal muscles in place, but lose the lip-rounding!
- Practise getting to and from this position.

  lloolloolloolloolloo llaallaallaallaa lleelleelleellee (etc).

- Listen to the quality of the sound you are making.
- Listen to us again…does your dark L sound the same?

So that's a dark L. Many accents use *only* a dark L: Scottish, the North of England, North America and Australia are all dark L only accents. If your own accent doesn't use a dark L, either because you only use light L or because your dark L is in fact a W substitute, you will be teaching your tongue a new shape. Keep practising the muscularity and sound until your tongue is confident.

If your new accent is a single L accent, life is pretty simple: you will need to use just one L all the time, be it dark or light. But there are many accents that prefer to mix and match their Ls (all of the South of England, for example). For these accents you need to know not only how to do each L but also which one to use when.

How to do a Light plus Dark L

For these accents you will need to be able to do *both* the light and the dark L!

The light L is only used if it is followed by a vowel sound.

● At the beginning of a word: **Look   Light**

● Separating syllables: **Toilet   Silly**

● On the end of a word if the next word starts with a vowel:

Hill‿and Dale   Fall‿Over

The dark L is used everywhere else!

● On the end of a word where no vowel follows it: **Hill**

● Before a consonant sound: **Field**

Listen to us using both Ls in the following sentence and then have a go yourself. Listen for the shift from light to dark L. We have helped you by indicating all the light Ls in *italics* and all the dark Ls in **bold**:

Larry the *lazy lamb slept peacefully* in the field until hailstones fell.

● Say these words using a light L:

Larry   Lazy   Slept   Peacefully

● Say these words using a dark L:

Field   Until   Hailstones   Fell

● Say these words starting with a light L and finishing each word with a dark L:

Lull   Little

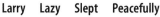

So that's the light L + dark L combination. This combination is an essential element in a Neutral Standard English Accent and many other accents in the South of England. If your own accent doesn't have this pattern there are two Ls to get your mouth around and you will need to be on your toes about which one to use when!

How to do a Light L or Dark L plus W Substitute Combination

These accents follow the same pattern as light L + dark L combinations.

> **The light L or dark L is only used if it is followed by a vowel sound.**
>
> ● At the beginning of a word: **Look   Light**
>
> ● Separating syllables: **Toilet   Silly**
>
> ● On the end of a word if the next word starts with a vowel:
>
>   **Hill_and Dale   Fall_Over**
>
> **The W substitute is used everywhere else!**
>
> ● On the end of a word where no vowel follows it: **Hill**
>
> ● Before a consonant sound: **Field**

Of course this pattern involves a whole new speech sound: the W substitute. So here's how to do it…

How to do a W Substitute

Listen to us saying the same sentence, only this time using the W substitute in place of the dark Ls.

Larry the *la*zy *la*mb s*l*ept peacefu*l*ly in the fie*l*d unti*l* hailstones fe*ll*

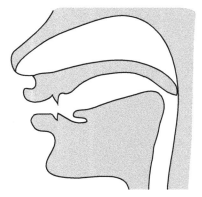

The essential quality of a W substitute is that the *tip of the tongue doesn't lift up to the gum-ridge at all.* The back of the tongue lifts as with dark L, and the lips round.

● Say the word **Well** and instead of saying the L replace it with the W you had at the beginning of the word, making an OO like sound: WE-OO.

● Make sure you *don't* use your tongue tip at all.

- Mouth the word silently, again replacing the L with a W.
- Do the above looking in the mirror and watch the movement of the lips as they round.
- Listen to the OO quality in the sound.
- Listen to the sound we used in the sentence (TRACK 21) and make sure yours sounds the same!

Practise the movement and sound on these words:

Hill   Field   Ball   Bottle

London is renowned for its use of a Light L + Substitute L pattern. Whilst in some accents of the deep American South you can hear a Dark + Substitute L pattern.

Practise the patterns on this paragraph, first using the London pattern; light L for the letters in *italics* and W substitute for the words in **bold**, then using the Deep South pattern; dark L for the letters in *italics* and W substitute for the words in **bold**:

> *L*arry the *l*azy *l*amb s*l*ept peacefu*ll*y in the fie*l*d unti*l* hai*l*stones fe*ll* heavi*l*y from the c*l*ouds. 'S*l*eeping is impossib*l*e!' he wai*l*ed. *L*assie the sheep-dog ca*ll*ed *l*oud*l*y: '*L*ift your *l*azy *l*egs *L*arry and come out of the co*l*d fie*l*d into this *l*ove*l*y warm she*l*ter'.

So that's the light L or dark L + W substitute.

You and The New : L

This sentence will quickly illustrate which L pattern you and/or your speaker uses:

Larry the silly lamb slept peacefully in the field until hailstones fell.

YOU

● What kind of L does your accent use?

● What pattern do you use? (Check the list below.)

Put your observations in the Major Players L section of the **You and the New Chart** on page 193. This way you will be able to see how any new accent compares to your own (photocopy this page, or download fresh copies at **www.howtodoaccents.com**).

THE NEW : the L Checklist

When you are working on any new accent use this checklist to be sure of this Major Player:

What L pattern does the new accent use?

1   Only light L

2   Only dark L

3   Light and dark L combination

4   Light L or dark L, plus W substitute combination

If the new accent uses a different type of L and a different L pattern from yours, practise the new L and the new pattern so that this Major Player doesn't *break* your accent, but helps to *make* it instead.

Listen to Track 17 to hear the different L patterns.

R L **H** NG TH

What makes H a Major Player is…

When there is an H at the start of a word some accents will say it ('H-doing') and others will not ('H-dropping').

Compared to the other Major Players H-doing or dropping is relatively easy, but it is no less important and still *key* to creating an authentic detailed accent.

Listen to these two speakers saying this sentence. The first is from *Newcastle* and is an H-doer; the second is speaking in a traditional *Cockney* accent and is an H-dropper.

Harry Hobson had a holiday in Hawaii

Say the sentence yourself in your own accent. Are you an H-doer or dropper?

H-doers

If you are *not* a natural H-dropper it is *really* worth getting on top of this feature. H dropping occurs in an enormous number of accents of English, and it is becoming more and more common. It can be heard in many regional accents of England and Wales.

H-droppers

If you *are* a natural H-dropper, you will need to focus on *replacing* those dropped Hs, so go to the end of this section for how to put your Hs in!

How to drop your Hs: some 'andy 'ints

This is what the words look like when you take those Hs away:

'Arry 'Obson 'ad 'oliday 'Awaii

They now start with a vowel!

Say these individual words, starting them with the vowel:

'Arry 'Obson 'ad 'oliday 'Awaii

Listen again to the whole sentence. Notice how with the Cockney speaker the words are *linked* from one to the next.

Harry Hobson had a holiday in Hawaii

The speaker treats the H-dropped word *as if it never had an H.* The words flow together just as they would with any word that started with a vowel. Watch out: a common mistake is for people to replace the 'missing H' with a glottal stop. Wrong!

The other lovely detail is: words that in standard English grammar would have had the indefinite article *'a'* before them now have *'an'*, as in this example:

A holiday becomes **An 'oliday**

Not all H-dropped accents do this. It is worth noting that in many young Contemporary 'Street' London accents, for example, this flow is disappearing, leading to a much more choppy staccato quality in the speech.

● Young Contemporary 'Street' London:

.arry .obson ad a .oliday in Hawaii

> **TOP TIP**
> *H-droppers sometimes aren't sure if a word starts with an H or not! They may think they dropped an H, when in fact they didn't. This can lead to a comic phenomenon known as **'hyper-correction'** when they put in an H which should never be there!*
> *Ask an H-dropper how to say the letter 'Aitch': they may well answer 'Haitch'...*

How to put Hs back in

Although H-doers may drop an H from a word that has no stress or weight at all, they would *never* do this if the word is stressed. Take this sentence, for example: 'It was his first offence.' If the stress is put on the word **first** then the H on **his** may get dropped: 'It was 'is FIRST offence'. But if the stress is on the word **his**, that H comes striding back again: 'It was HIS first offence'. If you are naturally an H-doer, you will follow this pattern too, but if you are not, getting that H to make an appearance may need a little concentration.

An H is just a puff of air, nothing more.

In Shaw's *Pygmalion*, Henry Higgins teaches Eliza Doolittle to put her H's in by speaking in front of a candle flame. As she pushes out the puff of 'H', she can see the flame flicker. Not a bad technique: try it!

You could also use a mirror, or a pane of glass, and watch it steam up as you push the H puff of air onto it.

- Put one hand on your stomach and the other in front of your mouth.
- Pant like a puppy. One hand will feel the muscles that do the pushing, the other will feel the warm air. That's an H!

Although this is pretty simple, it takes practice to drop this action into the midst of speech when you're not used to it.

- Try these phrases:

  I **h**ope so. I **h**ope you **h**ave.
  I **h**ope you **h**ave your **h**at.
  We **h**ave to. We **h**ave to **h**ide.
  We **h**ave to **h**ide in **h**ere.

4

You and the New: H

Said at pace, this sentence will quickly illustrate whether you and/or your speaker is an H dropper or not:

H: Harry Hobson had a holiday in Hawaii.

YOU

Are you an H-doer or an H-dropper? If you Drop, do you glide into the word as though no H were ever there? Or do you replace the H with a Glottal Stop?

Put your observations in the Major Player H section of the **You and the New Chart** on page 193 and put a note in the Glottal Stop section on page 194. (Photocopy this page or download fresh copies from **www.howtodoaccents.com**.)

THE NEW: the H Checklist

When you are working on any new accent be sure to check this Major Player:

● They only drop an H if the word is *unstressed*: they are H-Doers

● They drop an H at the start of a *stressed* word: they are H-Droppers

● If they drop, do they glide from word to word, as if the H was never there, or do they replace the H with a glottal stop?

Listen to Tracks 22 and 23 to hear the difference between an H-doer and an H-dropper.

R L H **NG** T H

What makes NG a Major Player is...

NGs can be Hard, Soft or Dropped.

And *which* one you use *when* depends on what type of word it's found in!

The kinds of words in which NG is found fit into two groups with distinct rules:

Group A – 'NG' Words

● NG nouns (people, objects) – a **Gong**; a **Singer**.

● NG verbs (doing words) – to **Hang**; to **Bring**.

● NG adjectives (describing words) – **Long, Strong**.

The rule? These can be hard or soft, but *never* dropped.

Group B – 'ING' Words

● ING verb endings (continual doing words) – **Running; Laughing**. (For the smarty pants amongst you these can also be known as the 'present participle'!)

The rule? These can be hard or soft, and *frequently* dropped!

A: NG words ——————————————

Listen to the two NG possibilities, hard and soft, on these NG words:

Gong   Singer   Hang   Bring   Long   Strong

● **Hard:** *Manchester*

With hard NGs you will hear a G or K quality on the end of the word.

(Found in accents of the Midlands and North West of England, and also in accents with a Slavic or Yiddish influence, for example.)

● **Soft:** *Essex*

With soft NGs you *won't* hear a G or K.

(Found in all southern English accents and all North American accents, for example.)

B: ING words

ING words can also be hard or soft, and they can also be **dropped**. Listen to these accent examples dropping the NG on the word **running**.

- **Dropped:** With dropped NG the action moves to the front of the tongue, making an N sound! But the fun doesn't stop there. Each accent will have its own specific sound that will fit one of the following styles:

  1 **runn'N** *Norfolk* (and Southern US States, Irish and Newcastle)

  2 **runnEN** *Wales* (and English South West and North West)

  3 **runnIN** *London* (South East England, Midlands, Yorkshire)

  4 **runnEEN** *Canadian* (Parts of Canada and America)

Running   Laughing   Dancing

Make sure you get the right kind of **drop** for your authentic accent.

The Patterns

The great thing is that many accents will pick and mix. This result is **four** possible patterns across the A and B words:

1 **Hard** in NG and ING words.

2 **Soft** in NG and ING words.

3 **Hard** in NG words and **dropped** in ING words.

4 **Soft** in NG words and **dropped** in ING words.

Which combination do you use? Does your new accent use the same? If not, learn the new sound and practise the new pattern.

Listen to us use each of these patterns in the following sentence:

The smiling singer was singing for the king.

NB: Accents that use soft NG in A and B words do in fact use hard NG-G but only in words such as:

- **Longer, Stronger / Longest Strongest** (comparative and superlative adjectives, adding an **-er/est** suffix to the basic adjective).
- **Finger, Anger, Jungle** (where the ending (**-er** or **-le**) is *not* a suffix, but is part of the structure of the word).

How to do a Hard NG

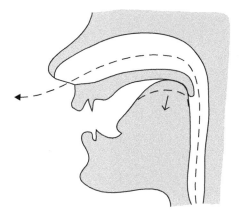

The back of the tongue is up on the soft palate.

It finishes with a squeeze that releases into the 'click' of a K or the 'bounce' of a G.

Complete the NG with a K or a G on all the A and B examples in this sentence.
(You'll see that A and B come together in the word **singing**!)

     B A   A B   A
The smiling singer was singing for the king.

4

How to do a Soft NG

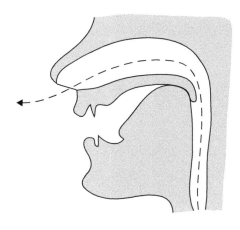

The back of the tongue is up on the palate and the sound goes into the nose.

The back of the tongue then has a soft release as it drops down silently.

If you are used to hard NG's then this will feel as if you haven't finished the sound!

Use a soft NG on all the A and B examples in this sentence.

Make sure you don't squeeze, click or bounce!

     B A   A B   A
The smiling singer was singing for the king.

How to do a Dropped NG

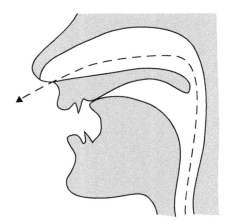

With dropped NGs the action of the tongue has shifted from the back to the front, effectively creating an N!

There are then two ways of dropping *into* the N:

1   **IN – EN – EEN**: There is an obvious vowel before the N and a clear second syllable.
2   **N**: There is no vowel before the N. The syllables crunch together.

Try dropping your NG's in each of these ways, but remember: only on the Group B/ING words.

B   A   A B   A
The smiling singer was singing for the king.

For some speakers (but certainly not all) dropping on the B words is optional, so that in more formal speech they will use whichever NG they use for the A words.

Practise the patterns:

Now you know how to do the sounds, practise the patterns!

1   **Hard** in A and B   2   **Soft** in A and B

3   **Hard** in A and **dropped** in B   4   **Soft** in A and **dropped** in B

> **TOP TIP**
> *Remember that it is important to break your brain's pattern of seeing a word and making assumptions of how you think it should be. Just because it looks like **NG** doesn't mean a thing-g!*

You and the New: NG

This sentence will quickly illustrate what kind of **NG** is used and when by you and/or your speaker:

        B A   A B   A

NG: The smiling singer was singing for the king.

YOU

- What kind of NG do you use?
- What pattern does your accent use? (Check the list below.)

Put your observations in the Major Players NG section of the You and the New Chart on page 193. (Photocopy this page or download fresh copies from **www.howtodoaccents.com**.)

THE NEW: The NG Checklist

Whichever NG combination you use in your own accent, the chances are that other accents use a *different* combination. When you are working on a new accent, listen for this Major Player and use this checklist:

What pattern does the new accent use?

- **Hard** in A and B
- **Soft** in A and B
- **Hard** in A and **dropped** in B
- **Soft** in A and **dropped** in B

If the new accent uses a different pattern from yours, practise the new pattern so that this Major Player doesn't *break* your accent, but helps to *make* it instead.

Listen to Tracks 24 and 25 to hear the different types of NG.

RLHNG **TH**

What makes TH a Major Player is...

TH is a sound that accents love to mess with. There are in fact *two* TH sounds in English, one made with voice and one without! Not only this, but accents will do different things with them depending on whether they're at the beginning, middle or end of a word.

Voiceless TH

THick   paTHetic   broTH

May be:
- **Standard TH**
- **Plosive TH**
- **T substitute**
- **F substitute**

Voiced TH

THose   broTHers   baTHe

May be:
- **Standard TH**
- **Plosive TH**
- **D substitute**
- **V substitute** (NB rarely used at the start of a word: **'ose brovvers not vose brovvers**)

Just like many of the other sounds we've looked at, these will work in patterns. Here are the five most widespread patterns currently in operation in accents of English.

The Patterns

1   **Standard THs** – everywhere (e.g. Scottish, most American, standard varieties of English).

2   **Plosive THs** – everywhere (e.g. many Southern Irish accents).

3   **T/D Substitutes** – everywhere (e.g. West Indian and *some* Southern Irish).

4   **Voiced TH = D** – at the start of a word, **V** in the middle and end. **Voiceless TH = F** – everywhere. (eg Contemporary urban English.)

5   **Voiced TH – dropped** – at the start of a word, **V** in the middle and end. **Voiceless TH – F** – everywhere. (eg Traditional London.)

Listen to the patterns in operation in these accents:

1 *Neutral Standard English*
2 *Southern Irish*
3 *West Indies*
4 *Contemporary 'Street' London*
5 *Essex*

It's a **th**ick pa**th**etic bro**th**

Look at **th**ose bro**th**ers ba**th**e

> **TOP TIP**
> *Although there are regional patterns in operation, they are constantly changing, and the pattern an individual speaker uses will be strongly affected by their generational and cultural influences. Listen to an example of your new accent to see what pattern **they** use. It may be one of the above or it may be a new one!*

Before you can do any of the patterns you will need to check you can physically make the sounds.

4

How to do Standard TH

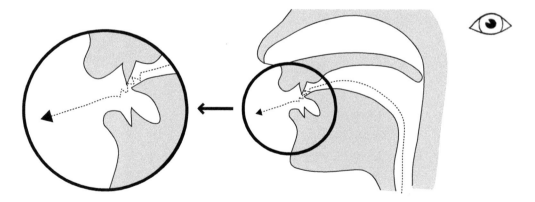

For the standard TH...

- The tongue almost touches the under side of all the top front teeth.
- The air is released with friction.
- Look in the mirror to see the tongue in position.

- Coat the underside of all the top front teeth *gently* with your tongue tip.
- Push air gently between the tongue and teeth and feel the air escaping. The tongue must stay soft to do this!

- Hear the air escaping with a hissing sound. That's the friction! That's your **standard voiceless TH**.
- Add voice to it (see page 89 – 'Feeling the Buzz') and you have your **standard voiced TH**.

Now try using the standard TH on these sentences:

It's a thick pathetic broth　　**Look at those brothers bathe**

How to do Plosive TH

When the contact between two articulators is firm you will feel the trapped air explode as they spring apart, making the sound a 'plosive'.

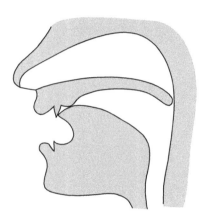

For the plosive TH the tongue is in *exactly the same position* as for standard TH, but the tongue is *pushed against* the teeth and the air is *not* released with friction, instead the tongue springs off the teeth, so now it's a plosive!

Look in the mirror to check the position of your tongue is the same as with standard TH.

- Push the tongue onto the back and under side of your top teeth.
- Keep it spread wide, just like a standard TH.
- Push against the teeth and bounce away in a T-like manner.

- The sound explodes, so you won't hear friction. That's your **voiceless plosive**.
- Add voice to it (see page 89 – 'Feeling the Buzz') and you have a **voiced plosive**.

So, for the plosive TH the only thing that changes from standard is the way the sound is released. This gives it a T- or D-like quality, but it's definitely not a T or D!

Now try using the plosive TH on these sentences:

It's a thick pathetic broth　　**Look at those brothers bathe**

How to do T and D Substitutes

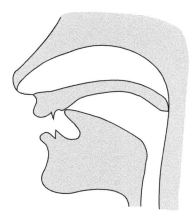

For T and D substitutes the tongue tip usually moves to the gum-ridge as in this illustration.

Replace all the THs with Ts in the first sentence and Ds in the second, making them on your gum-ridge:

It's a tick patetic brot   **Look at dose brodders bade**

How to do F and V Substitutes

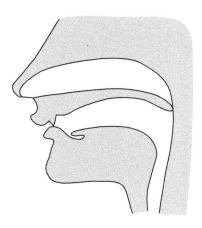

For the F substitute simply make a pure old-fashioned F.

Look in the mirror to see the top teeth tickle the bottom lip.

Replace all the THs in the sentence with Fs.

It's a fick pafetic broff

There's a twist, however: accents that use the V substitution only use it in the middle and ends of words, not at the start. At the start they will either use a D substitute, or they will drop the sound completely!

Replace the THs in this sentence with V, but drop the first one:

Look at 'ose brov**vers ba**v**e**

In fact, if there's one accent that can illustrate this it has to be Cockney! Listen to this example:

● **That's right, Bethany's with your brother!**

becomes

'As, right, Beffany's wiv your bruvver!

You and The New: TH

This sentence will quickly illustrate which TH pattern you and/or your speaker use:

TH: That's my brother with a thermos of Matthew's broth.

YOU

● What kind of TH do you use? Standard, Plosive, T/D Substitutes or F/V Substitutes?

● What pattern do you use? (Check the list below.)

Put your observations in the Major Players TH section of the **You and the New Chart** on page 193. (Photocopy this page or download fresh copies from **www.howtodoaccents.com**.)

THE NEW: the TH Checklist:

When you are working on a new accent, listen for this Major Player and use this checklist:

What kind of TH does the new accent use?

● Standard?

● Plosive?

● T/D Substitutes?

● F/V Substitutes?

And what pattern does it use?

1   Standard everywhere.

2   Plosive everywhere.

3   T/D Subs everywhere.

4   *Voiced* = D for the start and V for the middle and end of a word.
Voiceless = F everywhere.

5   *Voiced* = dropped for the start and V for the middle and end.
Voiceless = F everywhere.

Practice the new TH and the new patterns to be sure this Major Player doesn't break your accent, but makes it instead.

Listen to tracks 27-28 to hear the different THs and the different patterns.

THE MAJOR ISSUES

Consonants can be affected by these Major Issues:

- **Voice**, **Place** and **Manner** (how they are made).
- The **Glottal Stop** (where did that consonant go?).
- **Collisions** (dropping and crunching: when consonants collide).

The way in which accents play with consonants can differ enormously from one region to another. In some accents the consonants may be playful and soft; in others they may be sharp and precise. And as speech gets more rapid or informal they may disappear, merge together or even reappear as something else! *Junowo-ameen? Geddi?*

VOICE, PLACE AND MANNER

The way in which you make your consonants may be completely different from the way they are made in another accent.

Compare the *consonants* of these speakers from Liverpool and the Punjab and you'll hear what we mean!

Kate's taking me down town to a comedy gig.

> *Every* time you make a consonant you make three decisions:
>
> 1 How much vocal vibration is in the sound (**Voice**).
> 2 Where in the mouth the contact is made (**Place**).
> 3 The way in which the sound is released (**Manner**).
>
> Change one or more of these three elements and the quality of the consonant will change, which could move you from Liverpool to Bolton: a distance of a mere 36 miles, but a world apart in terms of consonant qualities.

There are 26 possible consonants in the English language. The chart below shows them in their *standardised* forms, using the letter of the alphabet that best represents them, and a simple word in which they appear.

- **Voice**: voiced sounds are shown in **bold**.
- **Place**: is shown across the top of the chart.
- **Manner**: is described down the side of the chart.

NB: The 5 Major Players are shown in grey. They have checklists of their own on pages 65 (R), 72 (L), 76 (H), 81 (NG), 87 (TH).

PLACE MANNER	Lips	Lip and Teeth	Tongue and Teeth	Gum-ridge	Behind Gum-ridge	Roof of mouth	Soft Palate	Throat
Plosive Air flow held back then suddenly released as a firm explosion	P B pip **bib**			T D tat **dad**			K G kick **gig**	
Fricative Air escaping continually, like a 'hiss'		F **V** fee **vee**	TH **TH** *thick* **this**	S **Z** Sue **zoo**	SH **ZH** me*sh* **measure**			H hay
Affricate Starts like a plosive but turns into a fricative!					CH **DJ** chew **Jew**			
Nasal Sound diverted down the nose	M mum			N nun			NG so*ng*	
Approximant Articulators brought almost together, then sprung apart	W wow				R raw	Y you		
Lateral Sound released from the sides of the tongue				L lull				

Voice: feeling the buzz

'Voicing' is a term used to describe the vocal vibrations present (or not!) in a consonant. (See 'Knowing your equipment', page 202.) Some accents, such as Irish, like to take voice *out* of many sounds, and some accents, such as Cornish, like to *add* it. The effect on the quality of the sound and the feel in the mouth is dramatic. Voiced sounds may feel soft, springy or firm, while voiceless sounds may feel hard, tense and sharp. Developing sensory awareness of the way sounds feel in the mouth makes doing accents a pleasure.

If you *remove* voice from the consonants in this sentence:

Good God, that dog has fleas!

...the effect will be something like this:

Koot kot that tok hass fleass!

While if you *add* voice to this sentence:

Some people say stop.

…the effect will be something like this:

Zome beoble zay zdob!

Have a go. Which one is most like your accent? As you do this you may feel and hear other accents emerging. When there is no voice you may hear the quality of Southern Irish, or German. When there is more voice you may hear the quality of the far South West of England: Devon and Cornwall. They may not do it all the time, and it may only be with certain sounds, but take notice if an accent favours **adding** or **removing** as their preferred quality.

- *Southern Irish:* **Good God, that dog has fleas**
- *Cornish:* **Some people say stop**

There are eight pairs of sounds in English which have a possible voiced (shown in **bold**) and voiceless (shown in *italic*) version. Listen out for these sounds and you'll get the most mileage out of this Major Issue.

The eight pairs are:

- **B** / *P* (Be / *Pea*)
- **D** / *T* (Do / *To*)
- **G** / *K* (Got / *Cot*)
- **V** / *F* (Vat / *Fat*)
- **TH** / *TH* (This'll / *Thistle*)
- **Z** / *S* (Zed / *Said*)
- **ZH** / *SH* (Measure / *Shone*)
- **DJ** / *TCH* (Gin / *Chin*)

Place: feeling the contact

When you say a T or D, where does your tongue tip go? Which part of the mouth does it hit? Does the tip touch the back of the top teeth? Or does it curl up to the gum-ridge? Or maybe it curls down and you feel the whole of the front of the tongue pushing against your teeth.

By changing the **place** where a sound is made, you can fundamentally change not only the way it sounds and feels, but also the whole muscular setting of your mouth. If the tongue is always having to curl up to the roof of the mouth or push forward onto the teeth, then over time, as we learn to speak, it will develop a specific shape in the mouth ready to move to this target. This then creates a muscular *setting* in the tongue. Try it on these sounds.

Say the following sentence in your own accent:

What a to-do to die today

Where does your tongue make contact to make the T and the D?

Now say the sentence again using these target points for your T and D. How do they compare?

● **Teeth**

    1   Bite your front teeth close together and push the tongue onto the teeth. (*Essex*)

● **Gum-ridge**

    2   Keep your teeth apart. Curl the tip up onto the centre of the gum-ridge and don't touch the teeth at all. (*Traditional RP*)

● **Behind the gum-ridge**

    3   Keep the teeth apart and curl the tip of the tongue up and back towards the roof of the mouth. (*Punjabi*)

As you move the tongue and change the target points in the mouth, you will begin to hear accents other than your own. Moving target points will change the tonal quality. As the target points move back in the mouth the resonance of the sound will get lower, and as they move forward it will get higher.

Make a T or a K on a whisper and move the target point gradually further back in your mouth: you will hear the notes drop.

Listen to us as we demonstrate.

Now listen to these three accents to hear the effect of the different placement of T and D.

  ● *Essex, Traditional RP* and *Punjabi*: **What a to-do to die today**

All that just from changing the **place** of your T and D! Any consonant can change its place in the mouth. The Liverpool K is way back on the uvula; in many Indian and Pakistani accents the L, N, T and D all curl way back behind the gum-ridge; and when many contemporary regional accents of England say the word **Death** the TH moves so far that it becomes an F.

> **TOP TIP**
> *Any accent you do will have its own set of target points that the tongue heads towards and its own muscular setting. The muscularity required may be very different from your own. Knowing where these targets are and feeling how the tongue gets there will help you to anchor the muscular setting of your new accent.*

Manner: feeling the release

When you make a K does it feel as if it explodes firmly out of your mouth? Does it feel splashy? Or full of friction? And what about when you make a TH? The way in which a consonant is **released** from your mouth will make a huge difference to the quality of the sound and therefore your accent. When the contact between two articulators isn't fully made, air will squeeze through the gap, producing friction and making the sound a 'fricative'. When the contact is firm you will feel the trapped air explode as the two articulators spring apart, making the sound a 'plosive'. Add an extra puff of air at the end and you have 'aspiration'.

Friction v Explosion

Listen to the *fricative* sounds the Liverpool speaker uses on the P, T and K compared to the *plosive* sounds of the speaker from just down the road in Manchester.

I can't **cook** a **pot**ato or a chi**ck**en.

And compare the *fricative* Scottish TH to the *plosive* Southern Irish TH.

That's the **th**ickest **th**ing.

As for adding an extra puff of air, many English accents love to put aspiration on their explosive sounds, giving them a 'hi-hat cymbal' quality, as this Essex speaker demonstrates. On the other hand there are those accents that love to remove aspiration, making the sound a little more 'bass drum' as our Punjabi speaker does.

● *Essex* and *Punjabi*: **K**ate's **t**aking me **d**own **t**own **t**o a comedy **g**ig.

From voice to place to manner, hi-hat cymbals, or big bass drums, changing the way your consonants are made; the amount of voice you use, where you place them, and how you release them, will dramatically change the way they *sound* and also the way they physically *feel* in your mouth.

TOP TIP

*Be careful: when consonants are different from our own there is a strong tendency to judge them, eg: 'Those are just sloppy, those are lazy, and those feel aggressive!'. That may be true for you, but it is **not** how the authentic speakers feel. Getting the feeling of the accent in your mouth will give you the physical experience of speakers of that accent, essential to sounding and **feeling** authentic.*

4

You and the New: Voice, Place and Manner

YOU

How does the way *you* make your consonants compare to the ***standardized*** forms in the chart below? Any noticeable differences? Are the differences in the use of **Voice, Place, Manner**, or a combination?

Put any significant observations in the Major Issues: VPM section of the **You and the New Chart** on p 193. (Photocopy the page or download fresh copies from **www.howtodoaccents.com**.)

THE NEW: Voice, Place and Manner checklist

Listen for how your new accent makes each of the consonants in the chart below (NB: the Major Players are shown in grey and have checklists of their own). Note any that catch your ear and are noticeably different from yours.

Is it the use of:

- **Voice** (track 31),
- **Place** (track 32-33)
- **Manner** (track 34-35)

or a combination?

Listen to tracks 30-35 to hear consonants being affected by Voice, Place and Manner.

PLACE / MANNER	Lips	Lip and Teeth	Tongue and Teeth	Gum-ridge	Behind Gum-ridge	Roof of mouth	Soft Palate	Throat
Plosive Air flow held back then suddenly released as a firm explosion	P **B** pip **bib**			T **D** tat **dad**			K **G** kick **gig**	
Fricative Air escaping continually, like a 'hiss'		F **V** fee **Vee**	TH **TH** *thick* **this**	S **Z** Sue **zoo**	SH **ZH** me*sh* **measure**			H hay
Affricate Starts like a plosive but turns into a fricative!					CH **DJ** chew **Jew**			
Nasal Sound diverted down the nose	M **mum**			N **nun**			NG so*ng*	
Approximant Articulators brought almost together, then sprung apart	W **wow**				R	Y **you**		
Lateral Sound released from the sides of the tongue				L **lull**				

THE GLOTTAL STOP

This is a sound that you will all know and recognise when you hear it, though you may not have known it had a name! The word 'glottal' means 'made in the glottis' (the area between the vocal folds) and the word 'stop' refers to the stopping of the air-flow. The sound it makes is that of a tiny cough or grunt!

A glottal stop!

The glottal stop is used in accents to:

- *replace* a T
- *accompany* a T, P or K
- *replace* an F or TH (but only if you're a cockney!)
- *replace* the word TO or THE

- *Norfolk:* **Pit Matter Frenetic**
- *Newcastle:* **Butter Paper Biker**
- *Cockney:* **Arthur Afternoon**

The glottal stop doesn't have an English letter to represent it, but it does have a phonetic symbol: **ʔ** (Yes, it does look very like a question mark, as though it is asking 'Where's the sound gone?': this is a handy reminder that it is often a *substitute* for a missing sound.) We will use **ʔ** whenever the glottal stop is being illustrated. 'Geʔiʔ'?

4

How to do a Glottal Stop

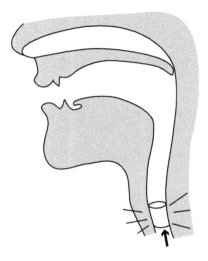

The sound is made in the **Glottis**, which is the space between the vocal folds. The tongue doesn't move *at all*. The vocal folds come together and STOP the air-flow momentarily. The air then 'pops' out when the folds open for the next sound, making a little grunt.

- Open the mouth and let the tongue tip rest against the bottom teeth.
- Make a tiny single cough sound and feel the 'pop' of air in the throat. That's a glottal stop!

How to replace a T

Use the cough of a glottal stop to substitute the T in these words. Don't move that tongue to make a T, let it lie flat!

- On the ends:

    Pit = Pi?   Hat = Ha?   Cut = Cu?

- In the middle (before unstressed syllables only):

    Matter = Ma?er   Glottal = Glo?al
    Kitten = ki?en   Frenetic = Frene?ic

- In-between:

    Get off = Ge?off   Might as well = Migh?as well   What if = Wha?if

Listen to our Norfolk speaker saying all the above.

Speakers that substitute T with a glottal stop are often aware that they do it, and can choose to replace the T if they want or need to. London accents are *very* versatile in the way they use this feature. A glottal T is considered the norm, but they may put the T back for emphasis or extra clarity (though it always lags a little behind!).

How to do a glottal stop accompanying a T, P and K

This is a lovely feature of accents of the North East of England. In fact understanding and recreating the unique way they treat the T, P and K collectively is *essential* if you want to have a believable North East accent.

Cockneys, East Anglians and some areas of Scotland such as Dundee and Kinross also do this for the P and the K, while using a full glottal replacement for the T.

In an *accompanying* glottal stop the tongue or lips only take up the *position* of the consonant P, T or K. The sound is *released* from the glottis.

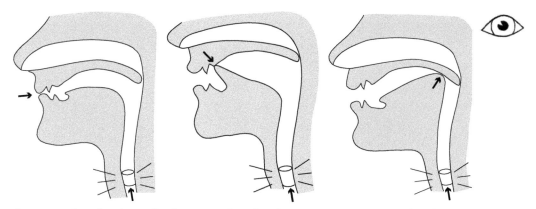

Accompanying glottal stop: P   Accompanying glottal stop: T   Accompanying glottal stop: K

(This may be hard to hear at first, but what you are listening for from our Newcastle speaker is a little extra beat *before* the glottal: it happens as the tongue and lips take up their position.)

● **Butter   Paper   Biker**

He put the butter in paper and gave it to the biker

- Go to say the word as if you are about to do the consonant.
- When you reach the position of the P, T or K, *freeze!*
- Hold the articulators in the P, T or K position but *swap your focus* to the throat and 'cough' the next syllable out.

Once you can do it slowly, try speeding up. This may well be a very new thing for your mouth to do, so don't rush it!

biker = bi?er   cooker = coo?er   baker = ba?er   talker = tal?er
paper = pa?er   wrapper = wra?er   copper = co?er

Once you feel confident, try using it in the sentence:

He put the butter in paper and gave it to the biker

> **TOP TIP**
> *Glottal stops are only used to replace or accompany P, T or K sounds at the start of **unstressed** syllables, as this word demonstrates:*
> *PARTICULAR*
> *The P starts the phrase, and the T starts the stressed syllable, so the only consonant that can be replaced or accompanied by the glottal stop is the C (sounded as K).*

How to replace an F or TH

Use the cough of a glottal stop instead of the F and the FT and the TH in these words. Don't move the lips or the tongue to make the F or the TH, let it lie flat!

Half in   Afternoon   Arthur

It's that simple: one challenge is believing it, and another is that it can make things difficult to understand. Treat it with caution!

How to replace the word TO or THE

In many accents of the North of England the glottal stop replaces the word THE, whilst in many accents of Scotland and the South of England it replaces the word TO.

'He's gone *to the* shop' becomes…

How to Do Accents

- *Essex:* **'E's gone ? the shop** (replacing the word TO)
- *Yorkshire:* **He's gone tu? shop** (replacing the word THE)

This is often written in playscripts like this: 'He's gone t' shop', 'On t' sideboard' – the apostrophe indicates a missing THE.

Try each because the effect and the feel is very different!
- **'E's gone ? the shop** (replace the word TO with a little glottal cough)
- **He's gone tu? shop** (it will feel as if you are saying the word TUT without the final T)

> ### TOP TIP
> *The **essential** thing is not to muddle these up. Make sure you know what the missing word is!*
> - *If the word is TO then it's a simple glottal*
> - *If the word is THE you say TU?*
> - *If you're doing a northern accent it would be daft to say 'Give it tu? me.' Because this would mean, 'Give it to **the** me'! Be careful...*

4

The glottal stop is on a bit of a roll in accents of English. It's spreading like wildfire, so that accents that never used to do it, or even frowned upon it, have picked it up and made it their own. Listen to all the different accent examples telling their stories (TRACKS 84-100) and we are sure you'll hear plenty of them.

You and The New: The Glottal Stop

YOU

Do you use a glottal stop to do any of the following…

- *replace* a T
- *accompany* a T, P or K
- *replace* an F or TH
- *replace* the word TO or THE

Put your observations in the Major Issues section of the **You and the New Chart** on page 194. This way you will be able to see how any new accent compares to your own (photocopy the page, or download fresh copies at **www.howtodoaccents.com**).

THE NEW : the Glottal Stop Checklist

Does your new accent use a glottal stop? If so, when? Is it used to…

- *replace* a T
- *accompany* a T, P or K
- *replace* an F or TH
- *replace* the word TO or THE

or in any other places??

Listen to Tracks 36-40 to hear the different ways a glottal stop can be used.

COLLISIONS

Consonants don't always stand alone in a word. Life isn't that simple. Consonants often collide or cluster in the English language: sometimes within a word as in 'a**ft**ernoon'; and sometimes when two words collide, as in 'goi**ng t**o'.

Accents often make life much simpler by *dropping* consonants out of the cluster (**elision**) or *crunching* the consonants in the cluster together (**assimilation**).

Listen to all these examples of consonants getting dropped from consonant collisions.

Where have all the Ts gone?
- I**t's** the be**st p**eople I mo**st** miss – **Is a bess people I mohs miss**

And what about this T and TH?
- Wha**t's** that – **Waasa?**

Where has this entire FT cluster gone?
- A**ft**ernoon – **Ah?ernoon**

Or this TH?
- He said some**th**ing – **He said sommingk**
- She's going out wi**th h**im – **She's going out wi yim**

And where are the L and R from this collision?
- A**lr**ight – **Awight**

As consonants collide they may even merge into one another, crunching together, sometimes changing one of the sounds, and sometimes making a completely new sound altogether. It happens to varying degrees in all accents, particularly as a result of rapid relaxed speech. If you say the phrase, 'How do you get to London Bridge?', it may surprise you to notice that many of you will actually be saying 'Londo**M** Bridge'. That is a consonant crunch! Accents may do crunches that your mouth wouldn't even dream of, and that's where the fun begins…

And here are some crunches for you to get your ears and mouth around. Look at how we've written the phrases, listen to the examples and then have a go yourself.

- *Essex:* Goo**d G**od! Wha**t do y**ou want? – **Goog God. Wochoo wamp?**
- *Manchester:* You've lo**st y**our ha**ndb**ag – **You've losh-chor 'ambag**
- *Glasgow:* What are you going to do? – **Wayeegundee**

And here are some of the most widespread consonant crunches, demonstrated by our *West Midlands* speaker:

- **DY**: Di**d y**ou do your **du**ty? (The DY crunches to J, as in Judge)
- **TY**: I'll pass that **tu**na over to you. (The TY crunches to CH)

- **STY**: I gue**ssed y**ou were **st**upid. (The STY crunches to SH-CH)
- **DR**: I had a **dr**eam about **dr**uids. (The DR crunches to JR)
- **TR**: The **tr**ain ran out of pe**tr**ol. (The TR crunches to CHR)
- **STR**: The **str**eet was ex**tr**emely **str**aight. (The STR crunches to SH-CHR)

Dropping and crunching may eventually become the accepted norm for a word, and so no longer considered an accent feature (as demonstrated by the word **cupboard**!).

> **TOP TIP**
>
> *When you listen to a speaker, in any accent you are working on, listen for any dropping or crunching when consonants collide. They will be most frequent in: unstressed syllables, fast speech and informal speech. If **you** drop or crunch but your new accent **doesn't**, beware! Don't infect your new accent with your own accent features!*

Lateral and Nasal Plosions

There are two extra special consonant collisions that are really worth noting. They are known in the phonetic world as **Lateral Plosions** and **Nasal Plosions**.

Sound uncomfortable? Well, if you're not used to doing them, they can be! They are an **essential** feature of many accents, such as a Neutral Standard English Accent, RP, Irish, Liverpool, and many others besides!

While describing these features in the accent of RP, Clifford Turner said:

> *a vowel should **not** be inserted between an explosive and a following L or N*

So what does this mean?

When the consonants **TN, DN, TL** and **DL** collide, either within a word, or between two words, the tongue goes up to make a **T** or **D** on the gum-ridge, and holds its position while either the sides of the tongue drop to release the sound from the sides (laterally) as an **L**, or the soft palate drops to release the sound down the nose (nasally) as an **N**.

There is no release at all between the two consonants!

Many accents DO insert a small vowel. In fact they often say it feels 'sloppy' not to.

Try these words;

little cuddle

What happens in your accent? Do you say **li-*tul* cu-*dul***, inserting a vowel, or do you say **li-*tl* cu-*dl***, using lateral plosions?

(NB: If you are North American you may be saying '**liddle**'. Try saying it with a T and see what happens then..)

Now try these words;

button hidden

What happens in your accent? Do you say **bu-*tun* hi-*dun***, inserting a vowel, or do you say **bu-*tn* hidn**, using nasal plosions?

If your accent *doesn't* use them, your mouth may not be familiar with these movements at all. They can feel, and even sound, quite peculiar, but they are an essential feature of many accents so...

4

How to do Nasal Plosions: TN DN

Drop your jaw, lift your tongue onto your gum-ridge to make a **T** or **D** on the gum-ridge, hold it in the **T** or **D** position while the soft palate drops to release the sound down the nose (nasally) as an **N**.

Hear It: Track 43a.   **See It:**

'TN'	**'DN'**
button	hidden
get nancy	had nuts

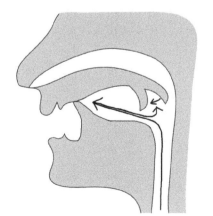

Feel It: The feeling is like holding a T while coughing down the nose!

When it happens within a word, there is no vowel between the consonants; instead the 'N' takes the weight of the syllable (syllabic 'N').

When it happens between words the 'T' or 'D' is held over and released into the 'N' of the next word.

How to do Lateral Plosions: TL DL

Drop your jaw, lift your tongue to the gum-ridge to make a **T or D**, hold it in the **T** or **D** position while the sides of the tongue drop to release the sound from the sides (laterally) as an **L**.

Hear It: Track 43a.

'TL'	'DL'
little	cuddle
get lionel	had lunch

See It:

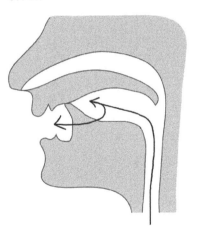

Feel It: The air explodes or splashes out sideways around the top teeth and cheeks.

When it happens *within* a word, there is no vowel between the consonants; instead the 'L' takes the weight of the syllable (syllabic 'L'). When it happens *between* words, the 'T' or 'D' is held over and released into the 'L' of the next word.

> **TOP TIP**
> *It's usually the TL and TN that people find trickiest, either inserting a vowel, or replacing the T with a Glottal Stop. Practise the action with the D, then change it to a T.*

And finally… T

'T' seems to act as a magnet for *all* the Major Issues: knowing what to do with it can quickly give you the tongue setting for your accent.

You've heard it getting dropped and crunched in consonant collisions – now listen to what can happen to it in Cockney in this one simple sentence:

There are three ways this speaker can say a T, depending on how he feels!

Pass the butter, Mum

- The first is an example of **glottal substitution**: bu?er
- The second is an example of **voicing**: budder
- The third is an example of **dental placement** and **aspiration**: buTTer

Crunching, dropping, voicing, glottalising, dentalising and aspiration are a key indicator of the setting: all this from one little sound! Now you can see, and hear, why overlooking the Major Issues could be a major mistake.

4

You and The New: Consonant Collisions

YOU

When you read 'Arthur the Rat' (pg 180) do you make all the consonants clearly, or do some get dropped or crunched?

Check this list of some of the most common crunches:

DY: Di**d y**ou do your **du**ty? (The DY may crunch to J, as in Judge)

TY: I'll pass that **tu**na over to you. (The TY may crunch to CH)

STY: I gue**ss y**ou were **st**upid. (The STY may crunch to SH-CH)

DR: I had a **dr**eam about **dr**uids. (The DR may crunch to JR)

TR: The **tr**ain ran out of pe**tr**ol. (The TR may crunch to CHR)

STR: The **str**eet was ex**tr**emely **str**aight. (The STR may crunch to SH-CHR)

Would you crunch all or any of these? Or would you never crunch any of them?

Lateral Plosions: What do you do with words such as LITTLE and MIDDLE?

Nasal Plosions: What do you do with words like BUTTON and HIDDEN?

Put your observations in the Major Issues: Consonant Collisions section of the **You and the New Chart** on page 194. This way you will be able to see how any new accent compares to your own (photocopy the page, or download fresh copies at **www.howtodoaccents.com**).

THE NEW: The collisions checklist

When you listen to a speaker, in *any* accent you are working on, listen for *any* dropping or crunching when consonants collide.

They will be most frequent in unstressed syllables, fast speech and informal speech. If you drop or crunch but your new accent doesn't, beware!

Also check for those Lateral and Nasal Plosions, and if you find them tricky…practise!

Don't infect you new accent with your own accent features.

Listen to tracks 41 – 43a to hear some of the dropping and crunching possibilities.

SPRINGING CONSONANTS

There are three consonants of English that can be termed **Springing Consonants**. In springing consonants (also referred to as semi-vowels) the articulators move *towards* each other, don't actually touch, and then *spring* apart. They are W, R and Y.

Because of this special quality they are often given a special job when vowels collide! A lovely little detail in some accents is the need for the mouth to insert a springing consonant to 'spring' from one vowel to another.

> Listen to these three speakers saying the phrase: **How are you?**

- *Lancashire:* In this example you can hear a **W** being inserted to push out the word **are**.

  How w-are you?

  You may think it's because there's a W in the spelling, but how muscular do you make that W? And what about, 'No idea'? There's no W in the spelling there, but still some accents really use the power of that W.

- *Cockney:* In this example you can hear an R being inserted.

  Haa r-are you?

  This may surprise you. But listen to the shape of the vowel being made in the word **How**. Because it is an open AA shape, the lips aren't ready for a W, instead this speaker prefers an R!

- *Belfast:* In this example you can hear a **Y** being inserted.

  High y-are you?

  Again, listen to the final shape of the vowel in the word **How**. It is close to an EE shape, so again the lips aren't ready for a W, so instead the tongue chooses a Y.

Each of these example accents finds the springing consonant (W, R or Y) that is *closest in shape* to the vowel they have just made, and uses this to spring into the next vowel.

> **TOP TIP**
> *Listen out for these springing consonants being used in any accent you are working on. They can add real authenticity to your sound and help you with the momentum and rhythm of the accent.*

SPOTLIGHT ON YOO!

The springing consonant Y often makes a special appearance before the vowel OO! When this sound appears as a speech sound in an accent, we will call it 'YOO'. (It may also be referred to as the 'liquid YOO' or 'YOD'.)

Most accents still use this sound, but when they use it will all depend on spelling! Take the words **Cute** and **Coot**, for example. We bet you don't say them the same way (unless you're from Norfolk, England!). And what about **Beauty** and **Booty**?

Listen to the words in this sentence spoken in an older upper-class RP accent, keeping all the Y-OO pronunciations (written in bold):

> Rather than be **le**wd, he pre**su**med it was his **du**ty to play a **few su**itable **cu**te **tu**nes **beau**tifully and with en**thu**siasm.

That's the sound!

> Let's start with some absolutes.
>
> This sound would *never* be heard, *whatever* the accent...
>
> - In words with O or double OO or OU in the spelling such as: **Move**, **Boot** and **Soup**.
> - After an L that has another consonant before it: **Glue, Clue, Blue**.
> - After an R: **Rude, True**.
> - After CH or J sounds: **Chew, Juice**.

(I know we said whatever the accent...but Wales is an exception! Welsh speakers have a 'flexible' relationship with this sound. They have a version of their own that is closer to I-OO than YOO. The only time they *wouldn't* use it is in the **Move, Boot, Soup** words. All the others may have it, or the English YOO.)

It is in all the *other* spellings that the fun begins!

What happens to all the possible YOOs in this sentence when *you* read it in your own accent?

> Rather than be **le**wd, he pre**su**med it was his **du**ty to play a **few su**itable **cu**te **tu**nes **beau**tifully and with en**thu**siasm.

...the chances are that they don't *all* have the YOO sound in them.

You are likely to be using one of the following patterns. You need to know which one pattern you use and which one your new accent uses:

1 YOOs everywhere.

2 YOO dropping after L and S.

3 Dropping after L and S and crunching after T and D.

4 YOO dropping after *all* gum-ridge consonants: S Z N T D L and THs.

1: YOOs everywhere

- *Old RP:*

  Rather than be **le**wd, he pre**su**med it was his **du**ty to play a **few su**itable **cute tu**nes **beau**tifully and with en**thu**siasm.

The only speakers that use YOOs everywhere (with the spelling exceptions noted above) are older, upper-class, RP speakers. This can make it a great 'period RP feature' for characters in Noël Coward plays and the like.

Here are just a few of the words you can have fun with in these accents:

suitable   lewd   sexual   absolute   suicide

2: YOO dropping after L and S

- *Yorkshire:*

  Rather than be <u>le</u>wd, he pre**su**med it was his **du**ty to play a **few** <u>su</u>itable **cute tu**nes **beau**tifully and with en**thu**siasm.

  (NB: 'presumed' may look like it has an S in it, but it's said as a Z!)

With the vast majority of contemporary middle-class English speakers the YOO has been lost after Ls and Ss. So all those lovely words above (**suitable, lewd, absolute, suicide**) no longer have YOO in these accents! (For reference, the OO sounds that were previously YOO are underlined.)

This only applies to stressed syllables, however. The YOO *remains* after the L in unstressed syllables:

- VALue

- SALuTAtions

And changes to SHOO after the S in unstressed syllables:

- TISHoo (tissue)
- ISHoo (issue)

3: Dropping after L and S and crunching after T and D

- *West Midlands*:

  Rather than be <u>l</u>ewd, he pre<u>s</u>umed it was his <u>d</u>uty to play a **fe**w suitable **cu**te <u>t</u>unes **beau**tifully and with en**thu**siasm.

If the regional accent is a little stronger, as well as dropping YOO after L and S, the vast majority of regional British accents will 'crunch' the YOO after a T, D and Z so that **tune** becomes **choon** and **duty** becomes **jooty**, and **presumed** becomes **prezhoomed**. This is a bit of a social class giveaway, so don't do it if your character is middle class!

4: YOO dropping after all gum-ridge consonants: S Z N T D L and THs

- *American*:

  Rather than be <u>l</u>ewd, he pre<u>s</u>umed it was his <u>d</u>uty to play a **fe**w s<u>u</u>itable **cu**te <u>t</u>unes **beau**tifully and with en<u>thu</u>siasm.

This is the pattern used by the vast majority of North American accents. In those accents *none* of the following words has YOO in it.

- S: **suit**   Z: **presume**   N: **nude**   T: **attitude**   D: **duty**
  L: **lewd**   TH: **enthuse**

And finally we need to make two special mentions.

The first concerns Wales. As we mentioned earlier, rather than inserting a Y before the OO, Welsh accents use a vowel close to E, making a sliding vowel sound E-OO. Listen to the way our Swansea speaker says the word **CURE** in her KIT LIST (TRACK 93) and you will hear this special sound. They may in fact use the English YOO in some words and the Welsh E-OO in others. Which sound they use when may depend on the age of the speaker, and whether there is a contrast being made between two words: for example, **Blue** has a pure OO vowel in Welsh English, but **Blew** has the E-OO slide.

- *Welsh:*

  Rather than be lewd, he presumed it was his duty to play a few suitable cute tunes beautifully and with enthusiasm.

The second concerns Norfolk. In Norfolk they *never* use YOO except at the very start of a word like *uniform*! (British readers may be familiar with a well-known Norfolk turkey company with the advertising tag line 'They're bootiful!'.)

- *Norwich:*

  Rather than be lewd, he presumed it was his duty to play a few suitable cute tunes beautifully and with enthusiasm.

(If anyone out there knows of any other accents with this pattern, please let us know!)

4

You and The New : 'YOO'

YOU

Read this sentence out loud. Which pattern of YOOs are you using?

> Rather than be <u>lewd</u>, he pres<u>u</u>med it was his d<u>u</u>ty to play a <u>few</u> suitable c<u>u</u>te t<u>u</u>nes b<u>eau</u>tifully and with enth<u>u</u>siasm.

(See the list of patterns and track numbers given in the checklist below)

Put your observations in the Major Issues: YOO section of the **You and the New Chart** on page 194. This way you will be able to see how any new accent compares to your own (photocopy this page, or download fresh copies at **www.howtodoaccents.com**).

THE NEW: The 'YOO' checklist

Listen out for words where the new accent keeps YOO when you would drop it, or drops YOO where you would keep it. They are likely to be using one of the following patterns. Make a note if it is different from yours.

1   YOOs in all possible places.

2   YOO dropping after L and S.

3   Dropping after L and S and crunching after T and D.

4   YOO dropping after *all* gum-ridge consonants: S Z N T D L and THs.

Listen to track numbers 46-49 to hear the four different patterns

And remember, this sound would *never* be heard, *whatever* the accent…

● In words with O or double OO or OU in the spelling such as: **Move**, **Boot** and **Soup**.

● After an L that has another consonant before it: **Glue**, **Clue**, **Blue**.

● After an R: **Rude**, **True**.

● After CH or J sounds: **Chew**, **Juice**.

So don't make the mistake of adding YOOs where they don't belong!

5

THE SHAPES

(Vowels)

IN THIS CHAPTER...

To do any accent authentically, making and using the right vowel shapes is a must. Learning the vowel shapes and sounds of another accent can take you straight to the heart of it.

We will take you through four steps:

- Getting the Big Picture
- Inventories and Distribution
- Shape, Length and Movement
- Getting more detailed

Did you know that every accent has its own set of distinct vowel shapes? Some accents have only five vowel shapes, some 12, while others have as many as 19. (Note that this has nothing to do with written English. We may only write five vowels but we may say many more!)

You'd be amazed if you could see what is really going on in your mouth as you shape vowels: it sometimes bears almost no relation to what you think you are doing! We may be aware of what is happening with the front of the tongue, but there's much more to the tongue than meets the eye: the tip does all the delicate work and the root keeps the tongue in your mouth, but it's the body of the tongue that moves to shape your vowels.

Surprisingly large, tongues can morph into all sorts of shapes like a big lump of modelling clay. The hump of the tongue can rise up and flatten down. It can undulate, like a wave. It can freeze and be held at a particular spot. And the lips join in with this too, rounding and spreading in tandem with the tongue. That's how we make vowels.

Each accent has its own set of lip and tongue shapes and movements, and in your own accent your mouth can find them instantly without any 'thought'. That's what you spent your time doing when you were a baby: learning *your* accent's vowel shapes and movements. As a baby you dedicated hours to hearing the sounds around you, playing with the shape of your mouth, until the sounds *you* were making matched the sounds you were *hearing* and/or *seeing*. You then practised those shapes and movements over and over again until they became *locked* into your muscle memory. That's what babies do. That's how you learned to speak.

To do *new* accents your mouth will need to find and learn *new* shapes and movements and thus *new* sounds. Time to unlock your old muscle memories and create new ones.

GETTING THE BIG PICTURE: USING A WORD LIST

People use vowels all the time, so you'd think it would be easy to hear what they are doing, but just when you notice one vowel, they've moved on to another and then another, and another! If you are trying to learn the new shapes, this can make life tricky. Hearing and mimicking words in isolation, however, enables the brain to calm down and focus on what it is hearing, seeing and feeling. This is where a word list comes in handy.

The phonetician J C Wells devised the following word list, known as the 'KIT LIST'.

1	KIT	7	NURSE	13	CLOTH	19	PRICE
2	DRESS	8	TRAP	14	THOUGHT	20	CHOICE
3	STRUT	9	BATH	15	NORTH	21	MOUTH
4	FOOT	10	PALM	16	FORCE	22	NEAR
5	GOOSE	11	START	17	FACE	23	SQUARE
6	FLEECE	12	LOT	18	GOAT	24	TOUR

NB: Please note that in older sample recordings you will hear the word CURE instead of TOUR as the last word on the KIT LIST. This is due to our recent decision to change the example word we use for this set. CURE and TOUR are the same set!

This word list can illuminate the three fundamental things you need to know about an accent's vowels: the **shape** they make, the **inventories** they have, and the way the vowels are **distributed**. (These terms are explained below.)

But before we get technical, why not let it speak for itself? Choose a reading of the KIT LIST at the start of each track from 84-100 that has a different accent from yours, or use your own resource recording if you have made one.

Listen to it once through. Do nothing, just listen!

Listen to it again, and this time mimic what you hear: just as with a language tape, repeat each word after you hear it. You might be surprised by what your brain absorbed from only hearing it twice!

Mimicking *accurately* requires good ear and mouth co-ordination. It is lots of fun for the brain to listen, absorb and copy. But be careful: the brain also likes to translate what it hears into sounds and movements it already knows!

Skip back to the start, listen and mimic again. This time listen not for what you *expect* to hear, but what you *really* hear! Pay particular attention to:

- Vowel shapes and sounds which are different from yours.
- Vowel shapes and sounds which are similar but not quite the same.
- Words that have unexpected vowel shapes and sounds.

Although you are focusing on shapes and sounds, this word list is in fact also giving you valuable information on the way your new accent organises its vowels, telling you how many vowels it uses and when. All this from 24 little words: magic!

INVENTORIES AND DISTRIBUTION

Sounds like a delivery service? Well, in a way, it is. In order to deliver your vowels to the right area, you'll need to know *how many* vowel packages you have and *where* they are going! (Be warned: this section can bamboozle when you first read it. Don't be alarmed! Read it as many times as you need. It's really quite straightforward, it's just the concepts that may be new.)

Inventories

> **An 'Inventory' is a list of the vowels used by an accent.**

Every accent has its own 'vowel inventory', a list of vowel distinctions recognised and used by that accent. An inventory is not concerned with *how* those vowels are made, just whether they exist or not. An inventory is really a numbers game. Some accents have only five vowels, some 12, while others have as many as 19!

When you listen to the Scottish (Glasgow) reading of the KIT LIST (TRACK 91) you will hear only 12 vowel shapes being used, some with an R after them and some on their own, but still only 12 vowel shapes. Listen to the Neutral Standard English Accent speaker (TRACK 98) on the other hand and you will hear 19 separate vowel shapes! Those are their **vowel inventories**.

Listen to these two example speakers reading the KIT LIST.

- Listen to how some of the Scots words use the same vowel: **FOOT** and **GOOSE** have the same vowel, **TRAP** has the same vowel as **BATH**, **PALM** and **START**. **LOT**, **CLOTH**, **THOUGHT**, and **NORTH** all have the same vowel: quite different from the Standard English (RP) speaker.

● And listen to the last three words. Because Scottish is a rhotic accent these are made with one of the 12 vowels plus an R. **NEAR** uses the **FLEECE** vowel. **SQUARE** uses the **DRESS** vowel, **CURE** uses the **FOOT** vowel. For the Standard English speaker we hear three new sliding vowels.

Countries can be divided up into 'accent inventory' areas. Scotland has a different inventory from England. The North of England has a different inventory from the South. The East Coast of America has a different inventory from the West, and so on. (Hughes and Trudgill have an excellent set of maps showing different accent areas in their book *English Accents and Dialects*. See page 220.)

The important thing is to know and use each of the vowel shapes in your new accent's inventory and you can identify this by listening to the KIT LIST.

If an accent shares the same vowel inventory as you the only differences you will hear in their version of the KIT LIST will be the specific *shape, length* or *movement* of those vowels. It may surprise you to know, for example, that HM the Queen and the Cockney Pearly King have the same vowel inventories as each other: it is the shapes and sounds they make for each of those vowels that are obviously very different. So for the Queen to pass herself off as a Cockney she would need to work on those vowel shapes, lengths and movements (oh, and perhaps the foundations, a few Major Players and a bit of the groove too!).

If on the other hand an accent has a very *different* inventory from yours, you will notice even more striking differences. The Queen and the Cockney not only have very different vowel shapes from a Scot, they also have a completely different inventory. They would have to lose a lot of their old vowel shapes, find a lot of very new ones and be careful not to let their old vowels slip back in!

5

Main Inventory issues

Let's cut to the chase. When you listen to the KIT LIST these are the most significant 'inventory issues' you will need to listen out for and get right in your new accent:

- **STRUT – FOOT**: One vowel or two?

  Southern English accents have two different vowels for these two words, but Northern English accents only have one, making these words rhyme.

- **FOOT – GOOSE – MOUTH**: One, two, or three vowels?

  Accents in England, Southern Ireland and America have three different vowels, one for each word. Scottish and some Northern Irish only have two, one for **FOOT** and **GOOSE** but a different one for **MOUTH**. Some Scots only have one vowel, making them all rhyme!

- **LOT – THOUGHT**: One vowel or two?

  Canadians, Scots and some Americans have one vowel for these two words, where other accents have two.

- **PRICE – CHOICE**: One vowel or two?

  For most accents these are two very different vowels, but for some rural English, West Indies, Irish and Newfoundland accents they are the same.

- **NURSE – START – NORTH – FORCE – NEAR – SQUARE – TOUR (CURE)** (All the words with R)

  For rhotic accents, note the vowel that *precedes* the R (eg **START** takes the **TRAP** vowel in our Southern Irish example, TRACK 90). For non-rhotic accents, note the vowel that *replaces* the R (eg **NORTH** takes the **THOUGHT** vowel in our Neutral Standard English example, TRACK 98).

Distribution ——————————————————

'Distribution': which vowels go in which words?

Once you are familiar with the set of shapes the new accent has at its disposal, the next trick is knowing which vowel to put in which word. This can be tricky. After all, if two words have the same vowel in *your* accent you may well expect them to in your new accent, but you can't be so sure! An American actress was doing a great 'Noël Coward' English accent in *Private Lives*, until she came to the line, 'I'm all damp from the bath.' She confidently announced, 'I'm all dAHmp from the bAHth'. It was a lovely English vowel shape, but little did she know that it belonged in Bath, but *not* in Damp. The Americans in the audience may not have noticed, but the English certainly did.

When it comes to knowing which vowel goes where, the 24 words on the KIT LIST are in fact more helpful than they look! Each word on the list represents a *whole set of words* that because of their spelling (and some history) will more than likely have the same vowel in it. For example, whatever vowel an accent uses for the word **CLOTH** it will also use for every other word in that group, such as **OFF** and **BOSS**; whatever vowel it uses in the word **STRUT** it will also use for **MOTHER** and **ENOUGH**. (We have provided lists of words found in each set with the KIT LIST on the *How to Do Accents* website, at www.howtodoaccents/kitlistsets. This is an invaluable resource. Though it is not an exhaustive list you will see patterns emerge in each group.)

Main Distribution Issues

And here's how to cut to the chase with distribution issues. When you listen to the KIT LIST listen to these words carefully. It is these sets of words that will have the most significant 'distribution issues' to watch out for in your new accent:

- **TRAP – BATH – PALM – START**

  Northern English speakers, for example, will use a short 'a' in **TRAP** words and **BATH** words, but a long 'ah' in **PALM** and **START** words (the vowel is lengthened to reflect the L and R in the spelling).

  Southern English speakers on the other hand only have a short 'a' in **TRAP** words. All the others have a long 'ah'.

  Rhotic speakers may have all sorts of variations for **TRAP**, **BATH** and **PALM**, but they pronounce the R in the **START** words which can seriously affect the preceding vowel!

5

● **LOT – CLOTH – THOUGHT – NORTH**

New Yorkers, Older London and upper-class English speakers have a short 'o' in the **LOT** words, but a long, rounded 'aw' in all the others.

Most other English speakers on the other hand, have a short 'o' in **LOT** and **CLOTH** words and a longer 'aw' sound in **THOUGHT** and **NORTH**.

And of course rhotic speakers may have one vowel in **LOT**, another in **CLOTH** and **THOUGHT** and yet another followed by an R in **NORTH** words.

● **NURSE**

Nurse words are a special category all of their own. They are derived from words with many different spellings:

■ **BIRD   NERVE   HEARD   FUR   WORD**

Historically this indicates that they were once pronounced differently, but over time they have merged into one sound. What is significant is that in Scotland and Ireland (both rhotic accents) the merger wasn't complete! Some speakers still distinguish the vowels in these words, using their **DRESS** vowel before the R in **NERVE** and **HEARD**, but their **STRUT** vowel for **BIRD**, **FUR** and **WORD**, for example.

It is worth pointing out that individual word pronunciation does fluctuate over time, and is affected by peer groups, social aspiration, etc. This can make words move from one set to another over time. For example, Standard English *used* to put all its **'trans'** words (translate, transport, transaction, etc) in the **BATH**, **PALM**, **START** sets with a long AH, but in recent times you will hear many speakers using the short **TRAP** vowel instead.

> **TOP TIP**
>
> *Once you know how a person says **one word** from the KIT LIST, the likelihood is they will say **all** the words from that group with the **same vowel sound**! This gives you invaluable information on the two basic structural issues around vowels: the Inventories **and** the Distribution. There are some good inventories and distribution maps of Britain, in Hughes and Trudgill's book English Accents and Dialects (see page 220).*

You and the New: Inventories and Distribution

YOU

Get to know your own vowel inventory and distribution issues. You can do this using the checklist given below. You need only do this once and it will provide you with a yardstick against which you can compare any new accent you work on.

Put your observations in The Shapes section of the **You and the New Chart** on page 195. (You may want to photocopy this page, or download fresh copies at **www.howtodoaccents.com.**)

THE NEW: INVENTORIES AND DISTRIBUTION CHECKLIST

Main Inventory issues:

STRUT – FOOT words: one vowel shape or two? (ie: does the vowel rhyme or not.)

FOOT – GOOSE – MOUTH words: one, two, or three vowel shapes?

LOT – THOUGHT words: one vowel shape or two?

PRICE – CHOICE words: one vowel shape or two?

NURSE – START – NORTH – FORCE – NEAR – SQUARE – CURE

- **Rhotic accents:** what is the vowel shape that precedes the R in these word groups? (eg START words take the TRAP vowel shape in our Southern Irish sample (TRACK 90). This makes START and TRAP one set.)

- **Non-rhotic accents:** what is the vowel that *replaces* the R? (eg NORTH and FORCE words take the THOUGHT vowel shape in our Standard English sample (TRACK 98). This makes NORTH, FORCE and THOUGHT one set.)

Main Distribution issues:

Do any of the words in these sets rhyme with each other? If so, they are one set.

- **TRAP – BATH – PALM – START**
- **LOT – CLOTH – THOUGHT – NORTH**

5

SHAPE, LENGTH AND MOVEMENT

Using the word list you can identify vowels changing from your own accent to your new accent, but can you tell in what *way* they changed? And can your mouth reproduce those new sounds accurately? If you are lucky your ear and mouth will co-ordinate easily: your ear will hear the differences and your mouth will make the correct changes to the shapes. However, they are just as likely *not* to! There may be sounds that are unusual to your ear and your mouth may simply not know what to do.

To make life easier for your ear and mouth it helps to narrow down what kind of changes you might be hearing and feeling. Accents distinguish one vowel from another through differences in shape, length or movement:

- **Shape** – Jaw? Tongue? Lips? How open is the jaw? What is the tongue doing? How round or spread are the lips?

- **Length** – Is it longer or shorter than your vowel?

- **Movement** – Are the jaw, tongue and lip shapes fixed, or do they move? If they move, how much, and from where to where?

Listen to these two people saying the word **GOAT** and read our descriptions of each, they are very different! Listen to them as many times as you like, and then try them!

Scottish: **GOAT**

- **Shape:**
  Jaw: Quite close together.
  Tongue: High at the back.
  Lips: Very round.
- **Length:**
  Fairly short/sudden.
- **Movement:**
  Held steady.

West Midlands: **GOAT**

- **Shape:**
  Jaw: Open at first then closing.
  Tongue: Starts flat, and then rises a little in the middle.
  Lips: Start relaxed then round.
- **Length:**
  Medium.
- **Movement:**
  Lots! Starts like A and ends like OO!

The Scot will have to make big changes to get that West Midlands sound and vice versa.

SHAPE: CREATING A VOWEL SPECTRUM

Okay…so we expect some of you are saying, 'What are they on about? I have *no* idea what my tongue is doing!' Believe us, you're not the only ones: it can be very hard to know what's going on in that mysterious black hole, and to work out exactly how you are making those sounds!

Open your mouth into *any* shape, let your voice come through it, and you've made a vowel. Change the shape (by changing the position of the tongue, lips and jaw) and you change the vowel. Try it. Compare the shape of your **GOOSE** vowel to the shape of your **FLEECE** vowel. They are completely different.

When it comes to making your own vowel shapes you don't have to think about what your jaw, lips and tongue are doing. The shapes and sounds are firmly fixed in your muscle memory, your mouth has learnt them and it knows what it's doing even if you don't! But there are many more vowel possibilities than the few that your mouth is familiar with. Finding these *new* vowels may mean exploring new areas of the mouth and co-ordinating your tongue and lips in ways they have never tried before.

Remember, there are just three things that shape a vowel:

- **Jaw**
- **Lips (and Cheeks)**
- **Tongue**

5

It is the *combined position* of these three articulators that makes each vowel shape unique.

Through teaching your articulators the **neutral setting** of the jaw, lips and tongue, and then creating a vowel spectrum using the eight most **extreme** vowel shapes and sounds possible, you can provide your ear and mouth with a clearer sense of geography and give yourself new reference points when listening to and learning the vowels of other accents.

Step One:
How to find a neutral setting

When the mouth is in a **neutral setting** the sound it produces is a neutral schwa (not your accent schwa, which may be far from neutral: see 'Setting', page 32). And it is represented by the symbol **ə**. It is produced from a relaxed jaw and un-rounded lips with the tip of the tongue gently resting against the bottom front teeth.

- **Jaw:** The jaw is released, but not open. This will mean that the back teeth are not touching, and the front teeth are apart, but not far enough for even your little finger to get in!
- **Tongue:** The tongue is lying flat in the bottom jaw, so that the slight hump in the middle of the tongue lines up with the centre point of the roof of your mouth. The tip of the tongue will just touch the back of the bottom teeth.
- **Lips:** The lips are neither round nor spread and the cheeks are soft.

Look in the mirror to check that all your muscles are relaxed and that the teeth are just a fraction apart.

Listen to the sound your mouth makes in this position. Add a little H before it, but don't change your mouth shape.

Now listen to us make this small, apparently insignificant, neutral schwa, as the unstressed vowel in the following words:

CommA   EddA   Above   thE

If yours was noticeably different you may need to neutralise your setting a little more.

Now you know where the neutral centre is we can anchor eight extreme vowel shapes and sounds in your mouth.

Step Two:
How to find eight extreme vowels on the spectrum

This will give your ear and mouth eight new reference points, radiating out from the neutral schwa in the centre, like this:

The Vowel Spectrum

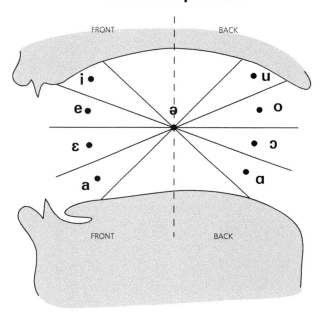

There are four reference vowels at the front of the mouth and four at the back, each labelled with a specific phonetic symbol.

When the body of the tongue makes a hump in the extreme point in each of these segments an 'extreme vowel' is heard. These sounds are also referred to as *cardinal* vowels.

Listen to us make each of the eight extreme vowel shapes, four at the front of the mouth and four at the back. Copy each sound as you hear it. (There is a more detailed step by step explanation of these shapes and sounds in 'Space Exploration' in Useful Stuff, page 208.)

You will hear them in this order: **i e ɛ a ɑ ɔ o u**

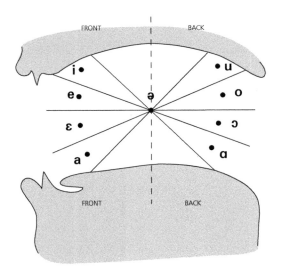

Jaw: During this sequence of vowels, what you can *see* on the outside is that the jaw moves from being close together for **i** to very open for **a** then close together again for **u**.

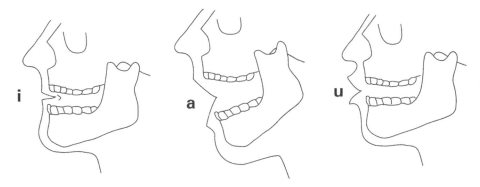

Lips: You can also see on the outside that the **lips** move from being spread for **i**, through to neutral for **a**, then round for **ɔ**, **o** and **u**.

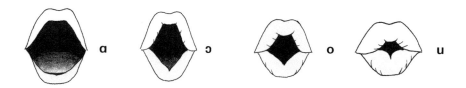

Tongue: What you *can't* see is that the **tongue**-hump starts high at the front of the mouth for **i**, flattens out for **a,** then lifts high at the back for **u**. This picture gives you an impression of just what the tongue is doing through this sequence:

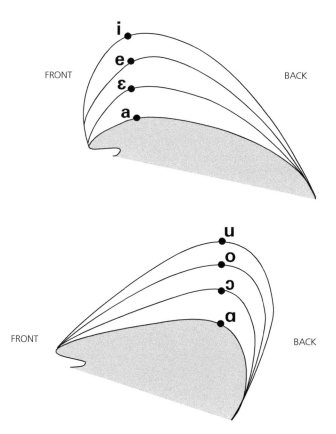

Listen as we make each of the shapes through the spectrum on a whisper. This way you hear the pure sound that the shape of your mouth is making, without the sound of your voice distracting you.

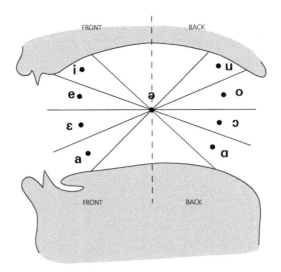

Listen again and repeat each sound after us on a whisper so that you can really feel what your tongue is doing. It can help to close your eyes to use your mind's eye to picture the tongue shapes.

Use your funnel (described in 'How to use this book', page 16) to listen to the sound of these whispered shapes.

As you make the sounds, it is important to visualise the *shape* of your tongue and connect the *feeling* of that shape with the *sound* you hear.

Look in the mirror to see the position and shape of your lips, jaw and, where possible, your tongue.

> **TOP TIP**
> *Watch out. Be precise. The brain is very good at translating what it hears into a sound or shape it already knows and making that sound and shape instead – don't let it!*

The result of all this co-ordinated jaw, lip and tongue movement is that the sound frequencies on this sequence go from very high and bright for the **i**, through the middle of the spectrum for **ɑ**, to very low and dark for **u**! It looks a bit like this…

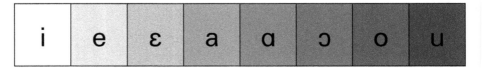

Now you have eight extreme reference points in your ear and mouth, shining a light into the darkness, giving yourself a sense of the geography and location of vowels in your mouth. This has developed your ear–mouth co-ordination, opening up many more vowel possibilities than the few that your mouth was accustomed to.

Once your ear and mouth are familiar with these eight extreme vowels you can begin playing with the effects of lip-rounding: adding or removing lip-rounding to each of the tongue shapes to give yourself even *more* vowel possibilities.

> **TOP TIP**
> *The more vowel possibilities you have available to you, the more accents you can do.*

How to add lip-rounding

- Make the *inside tongue* shape of **i. Fix it in place** and add the *outside lip shape* of **u.** (This will make the Scottish vowel in the word **GOOSE**.)
- Make the *inside tongue* shape of **ɛ. Fix it in place** and add the outside lip shape of **u.** (This will make the Welsh vowel in the word **NURSE**.)

How to remove lip-rounding

- Make the *inside tongue* shape of **ɔ. Fix it in place** and remove the lip-rounding to create the outside lip shape of **ɑ.** (This will make the Leeds vowel in the word **THOUGHT**.)
- Make the *inside tongue* shape for the centre point **ə. Fix it in place** and add lip-rounding to it. (This will make a Yorkshire 'hesitation' sound or accent schwa in **commA**.)

Listen to us as we do the above.

Accents and the Vowel Spectrum

As the hump in the body of the tongue undulates through the mouth it does not, of course, pass through solid lines that divide one sound from another. It works rather more like a rainbow. Where two areas meet, the sounds blend from one to another, providing a spectrum of vowels. A vowel may be halfway between **ɑ** and **ɔ**, for example: it may be on the borders, sharing qualities of both, it may move closer to the centre point or the extreme point, but you can only really know this when you: A) know what the extreme points are; B) know what they feel like; and C) know how they sound.

Here's what we mean: the vowel in the word **KIT**, for example, is made in the *general* area of the extreme vowel **i**, but specific accents may place it either very close to the extreme point or closer to the centre. The Glaswegian, New Zealand and Northern Irish **KIT** vowels (as in **'fish and chips'**) are good examples of this. In all of these accents the hump in the tongue is very close to the centre point and as a result the sound has some of the quality of **ə**.

Listen to these accent vowels and see where we have placed them in the spectrum. (The symbols we are using are the recognised phonetic symbols of the International Phonetic Association, or IPA.)

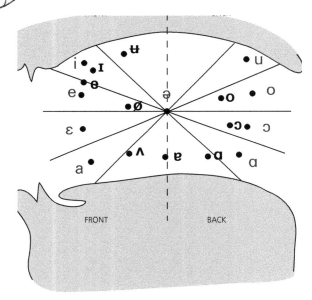

- The neutral centre point: ə
- *Cockney*: ʌ in **STRUT**
- *Glasgow*: ʉ in **GOOSE**
- *West Midlands*: ɪ in **KIT**
- *Manchester*: ɐ in **PALM**
- *Newcastle*: o in **GOAT**
- *Welsh*: ø in **NURSE**
- *Southern Irish*: e in **FACE**
- *Neutral Standard English*: ɔ in **THOUGHT**
- *Standard American*: ɑ in **LOT**

> **TOP TIP**
> *Remember your **Foundations** (page 27)? Get the foundations right and many of the simpler vowels will fall into place, leaving you free to focus on the tricky ones!*

You and the New: Vowel Shapes

YOU

The Kit List

Read out the KIT LIST in your own accent and write any observations about your own **shapes** (jaw, tongue and lip positions) on the **You and the New Chart** on page 195.

Vowel Spectrum

Photocopy the blank Vowel Spectrum towards the back of the book (page 208). You can also download a print-friendly version from **www.howtodoaccents.com**.

Read out the KIT LIST (page 179) and play 'pin your vowels on the map', putting your own vowels on the spectrum. Which extreme vowel are they closest to? Which are at the front? Which at the back? Which near the middle?

THE NEW: Shape Checklist

The Kit List

If you have a recording of your new accent reading the KIT LIST…

● Make any observations about each vowel shape (jaw, tongue and lip position) on the **You and the New Chart** on page 195. Now you can compare them to your own!

If you do not have a recording of your new accent reading the KIT LIST…

● Listen to your resource recording for any vowel sound that is significantly different from your own.

● Write down the word it appears in.

● Find the word on the KIT LIST that shares this new shape. (This will be the word that rhymes with it. For example, you may notice your speaker say SHOE with a very different vowel shape from yours. The vowel in SHOE rhymes with the vowel in GOOSE, so it belongs in the GOOSE set.)

● What is the new shape? How is it different from yours? Jaw space? Tongue shape? Lip shape?

Make any observations about this new vowel shape on the **You and the New Chart** on page 195.

Vowel Spectrum

Which extreme vowel are the new vowel shapes closest to? Which are at the front? Which at the back? Which near the middle? You'll see the places your new accent likes to go to and you can compare them with your own.

Listen to Track 54 to hear the extreme vowels on the spectrum.

LENGTH: LONG, SHORT OR IN BETWEEN?

The second way in which accents distinguish one vowel from another is through **length**. Within the list of vowel distinctions in an accent there may be some that are short and some that are long. Two vowels may be extremely close on the spectrum, but if the length is different it will be this that distinguishes them.

For some accents the **length of time** spent in one vowel shape is *crucial* while other accents aren't that bothered! New Yorkers are much fussier about their vowel lengths than many other North Americans, for example, and have strong distinctions between *long* and *short* vowels. Many Scots, on the other hand, prefer all their vowels to be short to mid length, taking the traditionally long EE (**FLEECE**) and OO (**GOOSE**) from South of the Border and shortening them, and conversely taking the shorter **DRESS** vowel and adding length to it – thus ironing out length distinctions.

> *Edda was working with a Canadian actor, playing a New York cop. His accent was great, he'd dealt with his 'oot and aboot', but when his character had to shout for the 'Doc' he headed back to Canada faster than a bullet from his gun! You see, Canadians love to lean into this 'Doc' vowel, keeping it long and steady, but New York cops are in a hurry, they use a short snappy vowel. He got the **shape** okay, but he just couldn't help using the Canadian **length**!*

Listen to:

- The short vowels of the *Scottish* speaker.
- The steady mid length vowels of the *Canadian* speaker.
- The long vowels of the *Norfolk* speaker.
- The switch from long to short vowels in the *Yorkshire* speaker.

Move that dog's poop off the grass, please.

A vowel may be short and snappy, long and generous, or somewhere in between. The vowel lengths have a profound effect on the rhythm and pace of an accent: it's always worth remembering the influence of geography, climate, culture, etc, on the rhythms and music of an accent. Of course, emotional intention can also affect vowel length. Accents that group vowels into long and short distinctions may make their long vowels even longer and their short vowels even snappier when the word is strongly stressed. And don't forget, the vowel lengths may be being affected by those surrounding consonants.

You and the New: Vowel Length

YOU

The Kit List

Read out the KIT LIST in your own accent. Listen and feel for the steady shapes. Some steady vowels may feel short or snappy, others may feel long or generous. Write any observations about the **length** of the shapes on the **You and the New Chart** on page 195.

THE NEW: Length Checklist

If you have a recording of your new accent reading the KIT LIST…

● Make any observations about the length of each vowel on the **You and the New Chart** on page 195. Now you can compare them to your own!

If you do not have a recording of your new accent reading the KIT LIST…

● Listen to your resource recording for any vowel length that is significantly different to your own.

● Write down the word it appears in.

● Find the word on the KIT LIST that shares this vowel shape. (This will be the word that rhymes with it. For example, you may notice your speaker say SHOE with a very different length of vowel from yours. The vowel in SHOE rhymes with the vowel in GOOSE, so it belongs in the GOOSE set.)

Put your observations about the length of this vowel on the **You and the New Chart** on page 195.

5

MOVEMENT: STEADY OR SLIDING?

The third and final way that accents distinguish one vowel from another is by keeping some **steady** and making others **slide**. By starting at one vowel sound and sliding to another you are making a sliding vowel, or 'diphthong'. The two sounds, the start point and the end point, effectively give the one sliding vowel two distinct halves, leading to these questions:

- What is the **start** shape and sound?
- What is the **end** shape and sound?
- Is each half of equal **length** and **weight**, or is one half weighted more than the other?
- How does the mouth **move** from A to B?

The sliding vowels are *great* value in accents. You can hear *extraordinary* differences between one region and another. There's just so much room for manoeuvre!

Nothing gives you away in an accent more than getting a sliding vowel wrong. The starting shape may be different from yours, the finishing shape may be different, and the way they get from A to B may be different too. It may even be that where you have a steady vowel they have a slide, or where they slide you're keeping steady!

> *Jan was working with a Welsh actor learning to do a Cockney accent. Just when he'd learnt to change his lovely Welsh sliding vowel in* **MOUTH** *to the Cockney steady vowel* **'MAAFF'**, *he had to change his steady vowel in* **FLEECE** *to the Cockney slide* **'FLuhEECE'**! *One size does not fit all!*

Almost *every word* on the KIT LIST has the potential to be either steady or sliding. But there are some words on the list that are *particularly* good value for money when changing from one accent to another, as the differences can be so extreme.

- PRICE
- MOUTH
- GOAT, FACE
- NEAR, SQUARE, CURE
- KIT, DRESS, TRAP, BATH
- GOOSE, FLEECE

Play with these and you will soon be travelling from Land's End to John O'Groats!

The PRICE vowel

This vowel can reveal *exactly* where you are from, better than a stamp in your passport! As with all sliding vowels, changes in the distance between the start and end shapes and the quality of movement from A to B will change the vowel completely.

> *We (Jan and Edda) both have a slightly rural 'squashed' quality to our **PRICE** vowels, and whenever we work together they seem to feed off each other making it more and more obvious where we're from. (Not helpful when you are trying to pass yourself off as a posh voice coach!)*

Listen to these examples saying the phrase: **Nice shiny bike.**

1   Small distance, gentle movement: *Southern Irish* **əi**
2   Medium distance, even movement: *Standard American* **ai**
3   Large distance, sudden movement: *Cockney* **ɑɪ**

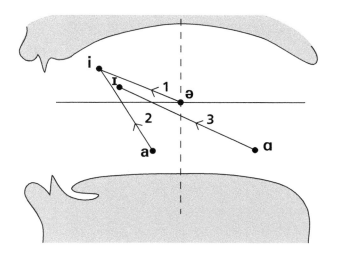

5

And what about weight distribution? Listen to these examples to hear what we mean:

● Weight all in the first shape: *Yorkshire*
● Weight pushing into the second shape: *Berkshire*

And listen carefully, because it may not slide at all:

● *Contemporary 'Street' London*

> **TOP TIP**
> *It's worth knowing that this vowel seems to have a built-in homing device. Maybe it's because we use it in the personal pronoun 'I', connecting it to our sense of self, who knows; but what we do know is that if you don't hang on to that new shape when the emotion kicks in, it will slide back to your own shape quicker than you can blink, and without you even noticing!*

The MOUTH vowel

This is another great vowel for playing with start and end shapes. There are so many possibilities!

 What happens if you make this **sliding vowel** starting from AH and sliding to OO?

- AH-OO: **How now brown cow**
- Now change the starting shape to AA: **Haa-oo Naa-oo Braa-oon Kaa-oo**

Here are some great accent varieties of this one sliding vowel for you to play with:

 1 *Dublin*

- E-OO: **Heoow neoow breoon keoow**

2 *Belfast*

- AH-EE: **High nigh brine kigh**

And remember…it might not slide at all:

3 *Essex*

- AA: **Aa naa braan kaa** (It's a steady vowel!)

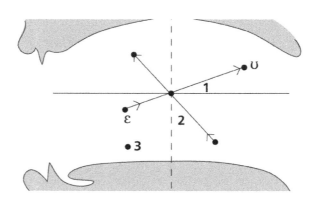

All that juice from one little sound. That's the power of the sliding vowel!

The GOAT and FACE vowels

If you travel in a straight line down the *middle* of Britain you will hear these sounds starting life as **steady vowels** in Scotland, gradually opening into small **sliding vowels** south of the border, and becoming larger and larger slides the further south you go.

Listen to these vowels travel from North to South…

● **GOAT**
  Scots
  ˏ*Yorkshire*
  Derbyshire
  West Midlands
  London

● **FACE**
  Scots
  Yorkshire
  Derbyshire
  West Midlands
  London

A similar thing seems to happen in North America too. In the North of Canada these two sounds are steady but by the time you are in Mississippi they are sliding like crazy.

You may even hear one accent start these sliding vowels with the shape another uses to end them. Listen to these diphthongs reverse direction from America to the West Indies:

● **GOAT FACE**
  1 America: **Guh-oot Fe-is**
  2 West Indies: **Goo-uht Fi-es**

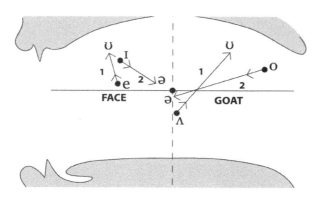

What do your **GOAT** and **FACE** do? You can bet they will have to change when you do another accent!

The NEAR–SQUARE–CURE vowels

The first thing you'll notice about these three is they all have an R on the end. That means that these three sounds are only sliding vowels in non-rhotic accents…and even then they may become steady! Confused? Here's a story that will clarify it all. Are you sitting comfortably? Then we'll begin: Once upon a time when all the world was rhotic, these three little sounds all ended in R. But some tongues got weary of regularly rearing and retracting, and so the R was weakened until it finally gave up altogether and all that was left of this once muscular sound was a tiny little schwa. And thus non-rhotics were born. Time marched on, and to this day the story continues. Some tired-out teenage tongues have even wearied of the simple schwa, leaving many young people with just a single steady vowel in place of that once muscular movement.

 Listen to us as we go from the R, to the **slide** to the **steady** version of each of these sounds.

- **NEAR**   EE-R   EE-UH   I…
- **SQUARE**   E-R   E-UH   E…
- **TOUR (CURE)**   OO-R   OO-UH   AW

CURE is especially odd because when it becomes steady it's a completely different shape!

The KIT–DRESS–TRAP–BATH vowels

These may not look like sliding vowels to many of you, but if you're from Belfast you may slide your **DRESS**, or if you're a Cockney you may slide your **TRAP**, and they could all slide if you live in the southern states of America. You might even put a Y bounce in-between!

- **TRAP** – trayup
- **DRESS** – dreyus
- **KIT** – kiyut
- **BATH** – bayuth

And last but by no means least…

The GOOSE–FLEECE vowels

Although these never become *huge* slides, they will often slide into position from a schwa, and the contrast between steady versions and sliding versions is very noticeable, as these examples comparing *Welsh* and *Cockney* demonstrate:

1   *Welsh*: **blue   goose   neat   fleece**
2   *Cockney*: **blue   goose   neat   fleece**

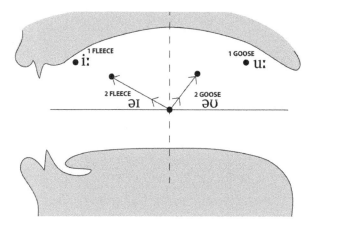

So, for *every* vowel the question is: is it steady or does it slide? And if it slides, learn its movement checklist.

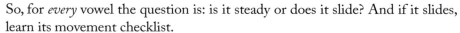

You and the New: Vowel Movement

YOU

Read out the KIT LIST in your own accent. Listen and feel for any sliding vowel shapes and make the following observations:

- **Start and end shapes** (eg FACE starts with my DRESS shape and ends with my FLEECE shape)
- **Length and weight:** Each half of equal length and weight, or one with more weight than the other?
- **Quality of movement:** A smooth glide or a sudden jump?

Write any observations about the **movement** of your shapes on the **You and the New Chart** on page 195.

THE NEW: Movement Checklist

If you have a recording of your new accent reading the KIT LIST…

Make these observations about the movement of any **sliding** vowel:

- **Start and end shapes:** The bare essentials!
- **Length and weight:** Each half of equal length and weight, or one with more weight than the other?
- **Quality of movement:** A smooth glide or a sudden jump?
- **Do they slide when you are steady? Or vice versa?**

If you do not have a recording of your new accent reading the KIT LIST…

- Listen to your resource recording for any sliding vowel.
- Write down the word it appears in.
- Find the word on the KIT LIST that shares this vowel shape. (This will be the word that rhymes with it. For example, you may notice your speaker uses a sliding vowel in the word SHOE. The vowel in SHOE rhymes with the vowel in GOOSE, so it belongs in the GOOSE set.)
- Make the observations given above.

Put your observations on the **You and the New Chart** on page 195.

GETTING MORE DETAILED: ENVIRONMENTAL ISSUES

So that's the **Big Picture**. Through using the KIT LIST you can gather the fundamental information you need on the shapes an accent uses, the distinctions it makes, and the way the vowels are distributed. Those are the basic essentials. But of course, in real life people don't simply read a list of words of your choosing, do they? (Shame!) They tend to speak in sentences, with words that aren't on your list and vowels surrounded by completely different consonants! Then what happens? Do those vowels behave differently in different 'environments'? A vowel is just like you; after all, you're a different person when surrounded by palm trees from when you're surrounded by concrete, and vowels are the same. They often behave very differently depending on whether they stand alone or cluster together, which consonants surround them, and whether they are stressed or not.

There are six major environmental issues facing vowels, and none of them is global warming! They are:

- **Nasal Colouring** (see below)
- **R Colouring** (see page 142)
- **The L Effect** (see page 143)
- **Free or Blocked?** (see page 143)
- **Stressed or Unstressed?** (see page 144)
- **Clusters and Collisions** (see page 146)

> **TOP TIP**
> *These environmental effects only become apparent once you know what the **basic** vowel shapes are. Only then can you listen out for them as they pop up in different places!*

5

Nasal Colouring

One of the things you *might* have been hearing as you listened to the KIT LIST is **nasal colouring**: a vowel being 'coloured' by nasality. It happens in many accents when the vowel is in the environment of N, M or NG. As the soft palate drops to prepare for the nasal consonant the poor wee vowel gets caught on the wave and disappears down the nose.

The most common occurrence of nasal colouring happens when the vowel is followed by N. As the tongue rises to the gum-ridge and the soft palate lowers, then off down the nose goes that vowel. You will also hear the whole *shape* of the vowel change as the N dominates it.

● *Essex/US:*   **Bee – Bean   Pat – Pant   Boat – Bone**

Some accents love nasality so much they do it all the time, and they do it with extra whammy near an N, M or NG. Listen to the Manchester accent example (TRACK 91). This is an accent that uses **Nasal Spill**. This sounds disgusting but it's really not – it just means that the soft palate is held low *throughout* speech as part of the basic setting, so that sound continually 'spills' behind and down the nose.

Some accents use nasal spill on particular vowel shapes, especially the **PRICE**, **TRAP** and **MOUTH** vowels, so clearly in order to do accents you need to have a flexible soft palate! (If yours is a bit sluggish have a look at 'Soft Palate' in Useful Stuff, page 205, for some basic exercises. If you need to do more work check out a good voice book such as the ones recommended in the Appendix, page 220.)

R Colouring

R colouring is a feature that will make your rhotic accents more detailed and authentic. It can be key to accents with strong molar and retroflex R's (see 'R' in Major Players, page 57) and it can really help you to distinguish one rhotic accent from another. It happens when a vowel is followed by an R. If the R is really strong, as the tongue moves to make it the vowel gets pulled along and 'coloured' by it.

R colouring is a feature of Northern Irish and many American accents, but it is not a feature of Southern Irish or Scottish. In these accents the vowel is said 'cleanly' and distinctly from the R that follows it.

Listen to the two speakers (*Southern Irish / American*) saying the words:
I heard the car.

● The *Southern Irish* speaker says the vowels *cleanly* and then *follows* them with the R.
● The *American* speaker starts moving to the R *immediately after the H and C* so that it swallows or dominates the vowels.

That's R colouring!

Vowels may be affected to different degrees in different accents. With the ER sound, as in **HEARD, BIRD**, etc, the R often replaces the vowel completely, whereas with other vowel + R combinations it may simply alter the shape of the vowel and pull back its resonance.

The L Effect

When a vowel is followed by a dark L or a W Substitute (see 'L' in Major Players, page 66), the whole shape may change. The back of the tongue rises up for the L and the vowel shape sometimes goes with it! Older RP speakers have the same vowel for **GOAT** and **GOAL** but younger speakers don't, and the London **FACE** vowel is completely different from the London **FAIL**.

> Compare the vowels in **pale** to **faced**, **goat** to **goal**, and listen to the 'e' in **felt** to **unwell**, in these three accents. That's the L effect!
> - *Old RP / NSEA / London:*
>   **The goat in goal was pale-faced and felt unwell!**

(And in the Cotswolds '-el' words (**Well, Elf**, etc) are pronounced 'OW'!)

Free or Blocked?

Vowels often change if they're left free to hang out, or stopped gently by a voiced consonant, or pulled up short by a voiceless consonant. Compare your vowel in these words:

May   Made   Mate

Are they all the same shape? Are they all the same length?

There are so many examples of this, and often it is just a matter of length, but Canadians take it to another level! Compare the shape of their vowel in **High** to their vowel in **Height**, and what about their infamous **Out** and **About**? You might think this is just their **MOUTH** vowel, but compare the shape when they say **Now** and spot the difference. Do the **Out** vowel in a **Now** word and our Canadian friends will have a giggle at your expense!

> Compare **out** to **now** and **night** to **sky** in this example:
>   **Go out now and look at the night sky.**

> **TOP TIP**
> *Vowels are **most** affected by the consonant that comes **next** in the word and these are the consonants that have the most impact:*
>   *N: PRAT – PRANCE   R: MAT – MARRY   L: GO – GOLD*

5

Stressed or Unstressed?

Vowels are not always stressed (unlike us!), and sometimes it's the vowel shape in those little unstressed syllables that will make all the difference to the authenticity of your accent. Word endings can be especially telling...

commA: Tiny though this ending is, it could make or break the authentic sound of your accent. What vowel shape do you use in these words? Round? Spread? Big? Small? What does your accent use?

Hear It: Track 71.

Listen to the final vowel in these commA words spoken in three different accents;

> commA   eddA

- Liverpool: **commE   eddE**
- Neutral Standard English: **commUH   eddUH**
- Cockney: **commA   eddA**

lettER: And in words with this little ending, is there an R (rhotic) or not (non-rhotic)?

If not, does it have the same vowel as commA?

If there is an R, is it heavy or light?

happY: and what about this ending? Traditional RP uses a KIT vowel, some Northern English accents use a DRESS vowel, whilst a Neutral Standard English Accent uses a FLEECE vowel. Which of your vowel shapes do you use here? KIT vowel?

> **TOP TIP**
>
> *Chances are that the shape of the commA vowel is the shape of the mouth as it relaxes back into its Foundation Setting (page 32). If you get this little detail wrong not only can it be a big give-away, but it also means you are losing the all-important setting of your accent that is keeping all your vowels in shape!*

And what about syllable stress? Listen to these examples of changes in stress patterns on CON and ILE words causing different vowel shapes to appear;

Hear It: Track 72.

- Northern v Southern English: **contain   concern   condition**
- English v American: **mobile   futile   fragile**

Suffice to say, listen out for those unstressed syllables to keep building a detailed accent.

TOP TIP

If you are North American there are two little sounds that can easily trip up your British accents.

The first is the unstressed final syllable in words such as *gentlemen*, *basement*.

In North American accents the surrounding nasal sounds colour the vowel and pull it into more of a KIT shape.

> gentleMIN   placeMINT

In most British accents there is no nasal colouring and the vowel used is a commA vowel, or schwa.

> gentleMUN   placeMUNT

Then there are those words that are *usually* unstressed and spoken with a commA vowel, or schwa, such as *of, from, what, was* and be*cause*. North American accents may use the STRUT vowel when they are stressed, but Standard English Accents the LOT vowel.

Hear It: Track 59.

> Of: 'Were you afraid **of** him?' 'There was nothing to be afraid **of**.'
> From: 'Who is that **from**?' 'It's from Jan.'
> Was: 'Who **was** that?' 'That was Edda.'
> Because: 'Just because you say so?' 'Yes, be**cause** I say so!'

5

Vowel Clusters and Collisions

And finally, what happens when one vowel meets another? Do they shake hands politely? Bounce against each other in a high five? Or do they interlock so seamlessly they become like one hand?

When two vowels from the KIT LIST meet head to head, new slides can be created, sometimes sliding through three or more shapes. For example, in the word 'created', the FLEECE vowel meets the FACE vowel, making a potential EEAY slide.

CREE- AYTED

This can also happen when a word ending is added such as ING;

GO-ING (GOAT vowel meets KIT vowel)

Or, in non-rhotic accents, ER;

PLAY-ER (FACE vowel meets NURSE vowel)

And it can also happen when two words meet...

GO OUT   DO IT   PLAY ON

The question is how are you handling these clusters and collisions? Are you;

Gliding, Inserting, or Smoothing?

Hear It: Track 72a.

tower   higher   going   lying

- **Gliding**: moving quickly and clearly through each of the vowel shapes.

  ta-oo-uh   ha-i-uh   gu-oo-ing   la-i-ing

- **Inserting**: adding a springing consonant, W, R or Y to bounce between the vowels, making a new syllable.

  ta-wuh   ha-yuh   go-wing   ly-ying

- **Smoothing**: ironing out the slide, partially or completely.

  taah   haah   geng   lahing

The extended word list

The extended word list below contains words designed to isolate the more detailed information on how the vowels and consonants might behave in different combinations and environments. It is by no means definitive, but it is a huge help in highlighting more detailed information for you.

If you only have this list recorded you can pick out the KIT LIST words from it (written in italics) to listen for the basic Inventory and Distribution issues before listening to the full list for the more detailed Environmental Issues.

It will also give you information on the Major Players, the Foundations and the neutral tune.

1	*KIT*	18	GIRL	35	TUESDAY	52	BEER
2	*DRESS*	19	BIRTH	36	*NORTH*	53	*SQUARE*
3	HEAD	20	BERTH	37	*FORCE*	54	HAPPY
4	NEVER	21	FLEE	38	POOR	55	LETTER
5	*TRAP*	22	FLEAS	39	*CURE*	56	HORSES
6	*CLOTH*	23	*FLEECE*	40	*THOUGHT*	57	COMMA
7	*LOT*	24	MEAT	41	MORE	58	WHICH
8	ONE	25	FACE	42	PAW	59	WITCH
9	*STRUT*	26	FAIL	43	*CHOICE*	60	SING
10	*FOOT*	27	STAY	44	*PRICE*	61	SINGING
11	BOOK	28	EIGHTY	45	PRIZE	62	GOING
12	*BATH*	29	*GOAT*	46	FIRE	63	NOTHING
13	FATHER	30	GOAL	47	*MOUTH*	64	BEETLE
14	DANCE	31	GHOUL	48	SHOUT	65	WITH
15	*PALM*	32	*GOOSE*	49	NOW	66	US
16	*START*	33	THREW	50	POWER	67	NEITHER
17	*NURSE*	34	NEW	51	*NEAR*	68	EITHER

5

You and the New: Environmental Issues

YOU

Do you use the following? Compare the pairs of words to identify your issues:

- Nasal Colouring: PAT and PANT
- R Colouring: MAT and MARRY
- The L Effect: GOAT and GOAL

And what about your Unstressed Word Endings?

- Happ**Y**: do you use the KIT, DRESS or FLEECE vowel shape?
- Comm**A**: What is your final shape? Round? Spread? Open? Closed?
- Lett**ER**: Do you use an R? If not, is it the same as commA?

Put your observations on the **You and the New Chart** on page 200.

THE NEW: Environmental Checklist

The possibilities of environmental issues affecting the speech sounds of an accent are almost limitless. Of them all, however these will give you the most milage:

- **Nasal Colouring:** Listen for words in which N, M or NG follow the vowel (*prance, ham, ring*, etc). Is the vowel shape affected by the nasal consonants? (TRACK 67)
- **R Colouring:** Listen for words where R follows a vowel (*heard, marry, cart,* etc). Is the vowel shape affected by the R? (TRACK 68)
- **The L Effect:** Listen for words where L follows a vowel (*old, help, sail,* etc). Is the vowel shape affected by the L? (TRACK 69)

And don't forget…

The Unstressed Word Endings

- Happ**Y**: do they use the KIT, DRESS or FLEECE vowel shape?
- Comm**A**: What is the final shape? Round? Spread? Open? Closed?
- Lett**ER**: Is there an R? If not, is it the same as commA?

Put your observations on the **You and the New Chart** on page 200.

Listen to Tracks 67-72a to hear some of the Environmental Issues.

6

THE GROOVE

IN THIS CHAPTER...

We will explore the 'music' you play when you create an accent. Every accent has its own music, made from a complex interplay of rhythms and tunes. Think about speech without music: it's robotic, it's just data, empty words. But with music we understand so much more. We know where the thought is heading, what's important and what's not, and not only that, we also know how someone feels about what they are saying. Just like music, each accent has its own distinct style, its own 'language of music'. This is what we call the 'Groove'.

In writing this chapter we are in some ways attempting to define the indefinable. Every accent has a way of using tune and rhythm that is unique, with hundreds of subtle changes, all giving equally subtle changes in meaning. Sometimes neighbouring areas claim to have very different accents from one another, when in fact the differences are really only to be found in the way they groove! However infinite the possibilities, it is possible to break this apparently complex structure down into a simple, step-by-step approach.

Begin by getting the **Big Picture**:

- **Frame it:** Put the cultural, historical and geographical frame around your groove to understand where it comes from.

- **Embody it:** Get a feel for the new groove by using Laban effort actions to anchor the physical dynamics in your voice and body.

- **Identify the Default Tune**
  Identify three characteristics of a basic statement.
  > Laban action
  > Default Tune
  > Musical Quality

Then add the **Detail:**

- **Intonation:** Within the overall features of the groove, refine your ability to hear and recreate intonation patterns.

- **Owning it:** Connect to the meanings the melodies convey and play them to express the actions, intentions and emotional journey of your character.

Don't forget, you've got a groove of your own, of course, which you do without even thinking about it! To do other accents you need to be able to change from your groove to a new one, to play a new 'language of music', and it can sometimes be a little trickier than you think.

A melody that suggests happy confidence in your accent may suggest rude superiority in another. The minor down-and-up slide of Liverpool is considered quite neutral to a Liverpudlian, but in Yorkshire it suggests a somewhat cheeky 'so what, who cares?' attitude.

So when a Liverpudlian actor Edda was working with was playing a boy from Barnsley, his own melodies were great for the scenes where he was being cheeky to his mum, but for the upbeat happy, confident speeches he needed to learn a whole new groove!

How to Do Accents

THE BIG PICTURE

Ever noticed that there is some music you love to dance to and some music that leaves you with two left feet? Picture the scene: you're at a wedding, there's a disco, and the DJs playing 'something for everyone'. You're having a bit of a giggle at Auntie Mildred and Uncle Stan as they struggle to keep up with the jerky rhythms and frantic pace of the hip-hop grooves, but then on comes a waltz, the tables are turned, and Mildred and Stan look like Fred and Ginger on the dance floor, a sight to behold!

The music we find easy to dance to is familiar: it means something to us. We recognise the beats, we know the moves and we feel safe in the groove of that particular song.

And it can be the same with the groove of an accent: some we will dive into easily; others we may have to learn step by step, just like learning a new dance.

Then imagine the children at the wedding: they seemingly find it effortless to dance to anything. They throw themselves into all the songs, playing and running around, unafraid of what they look like; they simply respond to what they hear and, more importantly, have fun with the new grooves. This is how we suggest you approach your accent grooves, with that same sense of energy and fun.

Frame it

What is it that gives each accent its unique groove? The groove of an accent is born of cultural values, historical legacies and geographical influences, and by framing your accent with these you connect the grooves to the people that made them.

The **cultural values** that lie behind an accent may be values such as frugality, self-reliance, hospitality, education or stoicism. These values influence the energy, rhythm and tune of an accent as it moves from moment to moment, from stress point to stress point through the thoughts and words of the speaker.

This is not to say that these are necessarily values that the individual holds, but rather that they are the traditional values of the community that have found expression in the music of the accent. For example, agricultural communities such as Somerset (UK) or Saskatchewan (Canada) need to take a patient long-term approach to life, so often these accents have a slower, more deliberate pace. On the other hand, city communities like New York or London value instant results, making the pace of those accents a lot faster. Yorkshire traditionally prides itself on its down-to-earth, robust approach to life and this finds

6

expression in the accent's weighty, no-nonsense tune and rhythm. Chants and rituals are an important part of Yiddish life, and the accents of Yiddish often retain this 'song-like' use of tune and rhythm. Very different cultures give rise to very different grooves.

The groove's **historical legacies** tell us something of the traders and settlers that have come and gone over time. There is so much to be learned about an accent by looking into the history of the people of the area. Ports are particularly susceptible to these influences. It is noticeable that some of the most striking accents of England are to be found in her busy trading ports. Scandinavian ports have brought their grooves to England, heard in the jumpy rhythms of Newcastle, and the sliding vowels of Liverpool, while the ports of England's West Country have taken their grooves as far afield as Nova Scotia and Barbados.

And don't underestimate the power of **geography** in influencing the way an accent grooves. In the far North of Scotland the often harsh living conditions give rise to a need for economy and stoicism which is expressed in clipped, staccato syllables, while the long dark nights give way to community story-telling, where dramatic use of tune and rhythm is a real asset! Accents from flat expanses of land such as Norfolk (UK) or Iowa (USA) often use a smaller range of notes with slower pace and extended vowels, whereas areas characterised by hills and valleys such as Wales (UK) and the Ozarks (USA) are noticeably dramatic in their range of notes and use of rhythm.

Finding your groove is about understanding where it comes from, what informs it and what values it expresses. Framing your accent in the cultural, historical and geographical influences that formed it will anchor the roots of the groove and provide a platform from which to take the next steps…**embodying**. Embodying will get those new grooves into your voice and body, and that means getting physical.

Embody it

Different grooves have different energies, dynamics and momentums. In order to explore these successfully we have found that nothing beats getting physical. Speech is a physical act. Taking a physical approach to grooves gets results. The body has an instinct for rhythm and tune that your mind may struggle to interpret. The voice likes to take its lead from the actions of the body. If you want to speak in a new groove, move your body or even just your arm in that groove and the voice will follow.

Actions derived from sports and dance – or other physical movements such as floating, punching, swinging, etc – have often helped us to get the groove into an actor's body, which in turn has helped them to understand and internalise the momentum and music of an accent.

> *When Jan was working with an actor from the RSC whose own Australian accent was leading to a narrow pitch range in his RP, they played with a chiffon scarf, dancing it around like Isodora Duncan, to encourage his range to find the swoops, floats and leaps of pitch used in RP. And when Edda was working with the actor from Liverpool who was playing the kid from Barnsley (see page 150), they played at shooting with a basketball to encourage his voice to leap up and over in the happy confident speeches, instead of sliding down and up. Although these actors had understood what they ought to be doing with the tune, and were both making fair attempts, it wasn't until they worked physically that they really got impressive results.*

Listen to these accents for the energies, dynamics and momentums at work and then have a go at them yourself. We've made suggestions for physical actions.

- *London:* Shadow boxing
- *Liverpool:* Slalom skiing
- *RP:* Swinging across monkey bars

These are just our suggestions. The important thing is for you to listen to accents in this way, to get a feel for the groove in your body and find your own physical metaphors to anchor the grooves in your body.

Another great way of getting the groove into your voice and body is to use a simple system of **physical dynamics**. Fortunately for us a movement expert called Rudolf Laban devised such a system for understanding the way in which a movement is performed! Laban identified three elements with contrasting polar opposites: space, weight and time.

- **Space**: Direct or Indirect
- **Weight**: Heavy or Light
- **Time**: Sudden or Sustained.

These elements combine to form **eight** different physical actions: GLIDE, FLOAT, DAB, FLICK, PRESS, WRING, PUNCH, SLASH. These **Effort Actions** are used extensively in drama schools to train actors to change physical manifestations of emotion. We took this idea and applied it to our accent work, using the actions as a shorthand for accessing shifts in the energy, dynamics and momentum of an actor's speech patterns. In one class we asked the students to classify each other's accents according to these actions. There was complete agreement: the Americans were PRESS, the Scots were DABS, the two from Yorkshire were PUNCHES. There was one student from Cork who was a FLICK, and there was even an Italian SLASH!

			SPACE	WEIGHT	TIME
		GLIDE	Direct	Light	Sustained
		FLOAT	Indirect	Light	Sustained
		DAB	Direct	Light	Sudden
		FLICK	Indirect	Light	Sudden
		PRESS	Direct	Heavy	Sustained
		WRING	Indirect	Heavy	Sustained
		PUNCH	Direct	Heavy	Sudden
		SLASH	Indirect	Heavy	Sudden

The ability to change the dynamics of your speech is essential if you want to do accents.

Do this next exercise in your *own* accent and notice which feel familiar; which feel different, but okay; and which feel downright weird…

- Listen to us speak the days of the week using each of the eight effort actions.
- Practise the physical action as shown in the table above.
- Speak the days of the week while performing the physical action.

Which one feels closest to *your* dynamic? This may be your accent pattern, or it may just be your own personal dynamic. Either way, become aware of it: it is probably a dynamic you use without much thought. To open your potential for doing other accents, learn to enjoy the other dynamic possibilities available to you.

So that's the actions. Here they are again. This time we have connected them to accents so that you can hear how to use them in this context.

Listen first then have a go at each of the actions yourself. Remember, make the physical actions as you speak; your voice will copy your body!

- *Standard American:* PRESS
- *Scottish:* DAB
- *Contemporary 'Street' London:* FLICK
- *Yorkshire:* PUNCH
- *Swansea:* SLASH

And how about these?

- *West Midlands:* WRING
- *Essex:* FLOAT
- *Southern Irish:* GLIDE

Exploring the 'Big Picture' groove in this way enables you to make big changes to the pace, rhythm, range and melody with which you speak.

> **TOP TIP**
>
> *Some grooves may have negative connotations for you. Maybe **you** only 'wring' when you are complaining; maybe **you** only 'punch' when you feel aggressive. Consequently, accents that have these grooves may feel whiney or aggressive to you. It is important to recognise this personal judgement for what it is and then put it to one side. What feels like an aggressive groove to you **doesn't** feel that way to someone whose own groove is always punchy!*

Once you have framed the groove and then explored ways of getting it into your body, the next step is to identify the Default.

How to identify the Default Tune ————————

Every accent has a Default Tune: a tune it will use for dispassionate information and simple statements of fact, with no subtextual meaning or implication: a 'news-reading' tune, if you like. This is a tune well worth identifying. It will set the 'standard', as it were, against which the other tunes of the accent will be contrasted. The Default Tune will have three qualities:

- Laban Action: a rhythmic, physical dynamic
- Default Tune: an over and down or under and up pattern
- Musical Quality: Major or Minor?

Hear It: *Track 76.* Listen to the intonation used by a Liverpool Accent and a Neutral Standard English Accent to make this basic statement, with no subtextual meaning or implication:

Susan bought a sandwich for me.

In Laban Action terms we say NSEA uses Dab and Glide. We might describe a Liverpool Accent, in contrast, as using Wring.

Now listen again to the way the tune moves.

The Liverpool Accent starts relatively high, travels **down** and then rises **up** again. We would call this an **under and up** Default Tune.

The NSEA starts relatively low, travels **up** and then falls **down** again. We would call this an **over and down** Default Tune.

 See It:

Liverpool: Under and Up	NSEA: Over and Down

LAUNCH	LANDING	tail	LAUNCH	LANDING	tail

Su san bought a SANDwich for me   Su san bought a SANDwich for me

This tune will also have a **Musical Quality**. If you were to write a piece of music that had the same quality as the accent, would you write it in a major or a minor key? While you listen to the tunes of various accents, you may notice that some tunes have a Major quality, while others have a Minor quality. Accents operate within differing pitch ranges within chunks of speech. Accents operating within small bands, with small slides between semitones and quarter tones may be described musically as having a Minor quality (West Midlands, Liverpool), whereas those that have the wider bands with steps between full tones may be described as Major (London, Edinburgh).

> **TOP TIP**
> *Accents that operate within the smaller bands can seem flat, repetitive and even whiney to people who are used to working within larger bands, while large band accents can sound overblown and patronising to those who use a narrow band: in fact they are neither, but this can have the beginnings of a culture clash!*

Now when we listen to the Default Tune in two contrasting accents we can describe it in these three ways:

	Liverpool	Neutral Standard English Accent
Laban Action	wring	dab/glide
Default Tune	under and up	over and down
Musical Quality	minor	major

So you've got physical, and musical, and explored the Big Picture. Now it's time to add the Detail..

THE DETAIL

In the last section we were exploring the 'Big Picture': getting the feel of the groove into your body, framing it with its cultural and historical roots, and identifying the default tune. This stage is about being more specific.

When you listen to someone speak, you hear **words**, which express literal meaning. You also hear **rhythm** to focus you on specific syllables, and **tune**, which provides more of the attitude and the emotional and subtextual meaning. The specific combination of rhythm and tune across a phrase of speech is called…

Intonation

- **Words**… This is just the words, you can hear the shapes and bite. Some of the accent is there but something's missing…
- **+ Rhythm**… Now I've added the rhythm so now you know which bits to focus on, but it still doesn't sound quite right… I sound a bit like a robot… There's one more thing to add…
- **+ Tune**… And that's the tune. The words and rhythm and tune combined are what make intonation. With all three together you have the whole accent!

As J C Wells in his book *English Intonation, An Introduction* (Cambridge University Press, 2006) puts it:

> **'Speakers of English repeatedly face three types of decision as they speak. They are: how to break the material up into chunks, what is to be accented, and what tones are to be used.'**

Of course, you make these intonation decisions entirely spontaneously in your own accent, but when you are learning a new accent you may well need to make those decisions in a more conscious way.

Every accent has its own patterns of intonation used to denote different pragmatic meanings. Many accents have very similar patterns, but with some you will notice that the melodies are significantly different from yours. The more unusual the intonation sounds to you, the more attention you need to pay to it.

Intonation is one of the first features of speech we learn as a baby. (Think about the way people talk to babies and dogs!) They are teaching them to recognise meaning not just in the words being said but in the intonation being used. 'It can take children ten years or more to fully grasp all the possible nuances of meaning conveyed by changes in intonation' (David Crystal: *Listen to Your Child*, 1986). You may have only three weeks to grasp those of your new accent, so refining your ability to hear and mimic intonation will clearly be an important skill.

Feel the Rhythm

Rhythm goes deep into our bodies and operates at a primal level.

Get into a person's rhythm and you stand a chance of feeling what they feel – ask Shakespeare! The interplay of stressed and unstressed syllables creates a basic rhythmic structure through every chunk of speech.

During a chunk of speech the intonation will operate a bit like a ball being thrown. Momentum is gathered up, the ball is launched, it makes a journey, it lands, and it tails off. The principal focal point in any chunk of speech is the Landing Point. This is last stressed syllable in the chunk.[1]

See it:

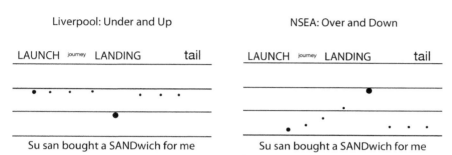

Feel It: Use your hands to clap out the rhythm so that you can hear it and feel it.

Some chunks begin with a **launch**; some gather on the first syllable and head straight to a **landing**. If you feel more than one landing point, chances are you have more than one chunk! Break the chunks up into phrases each with one final landing point. As you listen to speech in this way you will hear more and more of the possibilities.

Although any speaker may choose the same significant syllables or landing points in a chunk, and therefore the same meaning and basic rhythmic structure, the feel of the rhythms in accents can be very different. Once you have heard where the landing points are and have the basic rhythmic structure of a chunk, how does the momentum move from one syllable to another? This '**momentum**' will be affected by a number of things.

- Vowel Lengths: Short vowels will create a punchy, rapid rhythm (London). Vowel extensions on the stressed syllables together with reductions on the unstressed will create a very swingy, on-off rhythmic pattern (RP).

---

1 English is a **stress-timed** language. The stress determines the length of the syllable. Other languages may be syllable-timed. **Syllable-timing** is quite different. Although a syllable may be emphasised using a change in loudness or pitch, the syllable lengths will *not* change. Each syllable is the *same* length *regardless* of emphasis or stress. This means that you give weight to every SYL-LAB-LE, including small words such as **at, from, but, to** and **as**. This can often make the language and accent sound full and dra-ma-tic! Syllable-timed languages include: French, Spanish, Greek, Turkish, Polish, Hindi, Gujarati, Urdu, Punjabi, Bengali, Yiddish, Indonesian, Malay and many African languages.

- Consonant Strength: Strong consonants create weighty movement from syllable to syllable (Yorkshire). Loose consonants seem to merge the syllables together (Liverpool).
- Glottal Stops: Glottal stops create a staccato effect; the more there are, the more staccato the rhythm will feel (Newcastle).
- Suspension: The characteristic Welsh lilt (and Swedish too, for that matter!) comes when even stress is placed on two syllables and the voice 'suspends' between them.

It's also worth pointing out at this juncture that not all accents stress individual words in the same way. When words have more than one syllable there are choices to make. For example is it CONtroversy or conTROversy? Is it CIGarette or cigarETTe? Is it oFFIcial or Offi cial? Is it conSERvaTORy or conSERvatory? See what we mean? It may be that the new accent has different rules from yours regarding stress, and these rules can be tricky to identify. Here are a few examples:

Americans will always use some stress on those -ory, -ony, -ary word endings, where RP speakers never would. Word stress can change dramatically from America to the UK, so be careful!

In Northern English accents you will often hear more syllables in a word being stressed than in Southern English accents. Words with con- at the beginning, for example, such as concern, contain, etc, have one stress in the South of England, but two stresses in the North. This can often give the game away when a Northerner heads South, and vice versa.

Welsh puts even weight on two syllable words, such as kitten, and on the final syllables in a word such as eleven, and then also separates those syllables with a small hiatus (gap). This creates a lilting, choppy rhythm. You will also hear this pattern in some Scandinavian accents!

So, rhythm is created by word stress, sentence stress, vowel length, consonant strength, momentum and flow.

Now we have the words, and we have the rhythm, but we still don't fully have the accent until we have the Tune…

Play the Tune

It is only when you have the tune of a phrase that you will really hear the full accent.

As already mentioned, the landing point is the most significant syllable in a chunk. The purpose of all our melodies is to lead the listener to and from this landing point while also conveying a whole host of attitudes, emotions and subtexts. Quite a job! Before you take on the world, start with this simple process. To accurately hear and practise the melodic pattern of a phrase we find it really helps to detach the tune from the words, and then sing it. (Yes, we are serious!)

Listen to us extract the melodic pattern from a Belfast and a London example:

Listen to us 'singing' the tune. Notice how we slow right down to check we've got it right...

UNDER AND UP

Hear It: *Track 78.*

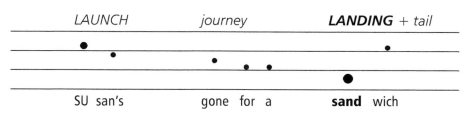

OVER AND DOWN

Have a go yourself at singing the melodic patterns of these two examples (you can do this with any chunk of speech from our sample speakers).

This takes practice and careful listening to pitch movement. When you're out and about, start listening to all the different tunes being used around you and seeing if you can sing them without the words (be discreet though or you might get a mouthful back!). If you have paper to hand, draw a rough musical score: our versions above use four lines (conventional musical staves have five lines, of course), which give plenty of scope to show pitch changes. As you do this you will notice that the rhythm and the melody work hand in hand. For some of you the rhythm may be your anchor, for others the melody, but be sure you are being accurate with both!

Owning It

One of the biggest mistakes that actors often make is to get stuck in Default. Can you imagine if you spoke in the same melodic pattern for everything you said in your own accent? Or if you just used two tunes – one for a statement, one for a question? It would be robotic and limited, to say the least! And yet we are sure you have heard an actor on stage, from time to time, that has got stuck in the default tune of an accent, using it over and over again, no matter what the subtext or emotional journey. Different melodic patterns are used to let listeners know if the phrase is a statement or a question, and also how the speaker feels and what kind of response may be expected. From the actor's perspective this is the element that expresses the Action of a line. Without variation and options all your actions will sound the same!

This aspect of intonation is often what seems to hold actors back, making them feel restricted when working in an accent. There are many degrees of 'knowing' an accent. Being able to truly play with all the possibilities in the melody will give you a real sense of freedom, fun and authenticity.

Some people are lucky enough to hear one or two melodies in an accent and then instinctively know what the other subtle possibilities are, but for many others it will take a little longer, and a lot more listening. There are so many possible subtextual expressions and actions, to shock, to disappoint, to inspire, to seduce, etc, and there are far too many to name. As an actor this is your emotional repertoire. Explore as much of it as you can in order to be fully versed in the emotional language of your accent. Within your own accent this aspect of intonation is second nature; moreover, you are emotionally connected to all your own melodies, they mean something to you.

When working in another groove it is vital to develop your emotional repertoire and make the same emotional connections to the tunes and rhythms of your new accent. Listen to as many chunks as possible on your resource recordings to identify all the variations your speaker uses and why. Below is a list of some of the more basic melodic variations you will need. If you are making your own resource recording try to get the speaker to demonstrate as many of them as possible.

Hear It: *Track 79.*

Definite Statement (default):

'I like fish and chips'

Interjections: These can have either positive or negative implications.

'Right…''Really…''Yes…'

Exclamations:

'I don't believe it!'

Tentative Statement: Implies you're not sure or there's something you're not saying! For instance, answering the question 'Is he attractive?' with:

'Well, he wears nice clothes.'

The tune would imply that he may not be that attractive!

Implicational Tone: Implies there's more to come (and often leads to a small encourager from the listener!). This is used for lists until the final item when the tune returns to the statement!

'He knocked on the door… (yes)… turned the handle…stepped into the house…'

Declarative Question: It looks like a statement but the tune makes it a question!

'We're leaving now?'

Yes/No Interrogative Questions: Questions that require a 'yes' or 'no' answer.

Q: 'Do you like peas?'

'Wh' Questions: Requiring more information than just 'yes' or 'no'.

Q: 'What time is it?'

Q: 'Where are you?'

Q: 'When did you arrive?'

Q: 'Who's there?'

Q: 'Why are you laughing?'

Q: 'How old are you?'

Tags: Short additions added to the end of a phrase to either:

A Ask for confirmation: 'We've been here before, haven't we?'

B Declare expected agreement: 'We've been here before, haven't we.'

Command:

'Put that down!'

6

(See our other book *How To Do Standard English Accents* for ten broad, but really useful LAUNCH and LAND combinations in a Neutral Standard English Accent!)

You and The New: the Groove

YOU

Laban Action: Which action, or actions, best describes the rhythm and momentum of your accent? (TRACKS 74-75)

Default Tune: When making a statement of fact which of the following do you do?

- UNDER and UP: stress the main word UNDER the rest of the phrase, with the tail of the phrase rising UP. (TRACK 77)
- OVER and DOWN: stress the main word OVER the rest of the phrase, with the tail of the phrase falling DOWN. (TRACK 77)

Musical Quality: Do your tunes have a Major or Minor quality? And do you step up and down, or slide between the notes in a phrase?

Put these and any other observations on the way your accent grooves in the Groove section of the **You and the New Chart** on page 200. This way you will be able to see how any new accent compares to your own. (Photocopy the page, or download fresh copies at **www.howtodoaccents.com.**)

THE NEW: the groove checklist

Laban Action: Which Laban action (or actions) best describe(s) the rhythm and momentum of the new accent? How does this compare to your own? (TRACKS 74-75)

Default Tune: When making a statement of fact which of the following does the new accent do? Is it like yours?

- UNDER and UP: stress the main word UNDER the rest of the phrase, with the tail of the phrase rising UP. (TRACK 76)
- OVER and DOWN: stress the main word OVER the rest of the phrase, with the tail of the phrase falling DOWN. (TRACK 76)

Musical Quality: Do the tunes they use have a Major or Minor quality? And do they step up and down, or slide between the notes in a phrase? How does this compare to your groove?

Listen to Tracks 74 and 75 to hear the Laban Actions.

Listen to Track 77 to hear the tune going UNDER and OVER.

Listen for any catchy tunes the new accent uses and make a note of them in the blank melody section of the You and the New chart on page 201.

7

GET PROFESSIONAL

IN THIS CHAPTER...

Assuming you aren't simply doing accents as a hobby, you will also need to know how to take your work in the professional arena to a professional level. This means knowing not just how to **do** an accent, but also how to **work on** it to keep improving it and how to **work with** it in different professional contexts.

First of all we will give you advice on how to **get practising**: after all, if you want to be professional at something you have to practise.

We then take you through what to do when your accent meets the specific demands of:

- the production
- the director
- the rehearsal
- the character.

And finally:

- How to handle an audition
- How to handle sight-reading.

GET PRACTISING

It ought to go without saying (but it often doesn't) that if you want to be good at something it takes practice. This doesn't mean having to sit for hours labouring over your script: it simply means building a little bit of accent practice into your daily routine.

It is absolutely essential to practise both on and off your text. If the only things you can say in the accent are the words in your script, you do not know the accent and your performance will be limited. What happens when someone forgets their cue and you have to ad lib? Or there's a re-write, or a cut reappears? You're scuppered!

So, here's our advice for accent practice.

Springboard sentence

- Have a 'springboard sentence' in the accent. This is a short phrase that automatically gets the accent into your mouth, seemingly without you being involved. Your brain associates that phrase with the accent and as soon as you say it that 'accent file' in your head downloads and opens up. This is invaluable for those moments when you seem to go adrift and need to 'reboot' the accent.

Out in the real world

- Read billboards, adverts, notices and other short bursts of text either out loud or in your head. This trains you to translate from the written word into the new spoken patterns of an accent.

- Look out for specific sounds and see if you can identify them on billboards, etc.

- Ask for directions, or for assistance in a shop.

7

Anytime, anywhere

- Listen to your accent resource a little every day. You can do this while you're getting a meal ready, in the car, at the gym, even as you go to sleep; anywhere that makes it easy and regular. It is vital to give your brain something to refer to and feed off (see 'Making your own resource recording' in Getting Started, page 23).

● Narrate your day: 'I think I'll just put the kettle on', 'Oh, that's the phone, I'll just answer it', and so on. Notice and correct any mistakes as you make them. It's crucial not to reinforce bad habits but to teach yourself the new patterns. Horsey types will tell you that if you let a horse refuse a jump once the chances are it will refuse it again, and we can tell you that your mouth behaves in much the same way. Remember just like the rider, you are the one in charge, not your mouth, so make sure you *always* correct it at every jump!

● If there's a group of you learning the accent, have an accent evening: you could cook the food, listen to the music, watch the movies, whatever takes your fancy. Any excuse for a party!

● Don't just practise the bits you're good at. Focus on different elements of the accent – the Foundations, the Major Players, vowel Shapes or the Groove.

With the Set Text

● Practise with the Set Text ('Arthur the Rat') and KIT LIST provided in Useful Stuff (pages 179–80). The Set Text contains all the sounds and combinations of the sounds in English, so once you can say this you can say everything!

● Record yourself. Play it back and be your own judge. If you don't convince yourself you won't convince anyone else either!

● If you used the Set Text to make your own resource recording, play it frequently while you read and speak along with it. You will learn so much in terms of the specific articulation of vowels, consonants and combinations, and also in the overall use of energy, tune, etc.

● The more you work with the Set Text and the KIT LIST, the more you will get to know them. Once you can confidently recite them in the accent they will be invaluable as warm-up and practice material.

On the script

Eventually, of course, your words will be connected to emotional impulses and actions, but there is also a certain amount of basic technical **gymnastics** that your mouth is going to have to get used to before you get there. This may be more or less challenging depending on the accent you are doing and your familiarity with it. Sometimes you need to let yourself off the 'emotional' hook and work on your script technically. This is only the same as doing table work and blocking in rehearsals. You do it with the acting, so do it with the accent.

- To begin with you may want to read very slowly out loud in your new accent, a little like a child learning to read, plotting your way through the sounds.

- Work on your text phrase by phrase.

- Identify words in the phrase that can take the stress. These will provide anchor sounds in the phrase. These stresses are only temporary, as things may change during rehearsals, but you need them as a starting point. Practise these words first so that you are confident in making the shapes and sounds. They will provide solid stepping stones through the text.

Practising your text is very much like practising a **gymnastics tumbling routine**. To begin with, you have to practise each of the moves separately before you can string them together. Once you are confident you stand at one corner of the floor mat, looking at the 'phrase' to be performed between there and the far corner. You breathe and… GO!…, landing with aplomb at the far corner. If anything does go wrong you know that bit needs reworking until the whole sequence is flawless. These are the steps:

1 Identify the 'big moves' in the routine – the triple sukahara, the double back flip and the handspring! These may be words you find tricky, or specific vowels or consonant combinations.

2 Work on each of these moves separately until your mouth can do them smoothly.

3 Practise getting both to and from each of these moves until you can get through the whole phrase fluently. If you falter, stumble or trip, keep going back to step two until you can say the whole phrase without tripping.

4 Once you are confident with the technical aspect of the gymnastics the next step for a perfect 10 is to do it 'once more with feeling'. If when you connect to the emotional drive of the line things begin to slip, go back and look at those bits again. Connect the sound firmly to the feeling so that the two things becomes one.

7

> **TOP TIP**
> *You only really know your lines when you can say them…*
> ● *technically*
> ● *fluently*
> ● *emotionally.*

ACCENT MEETS PRODUCTION

Over the years we have worked with many different kinds of actor and director, each with their own working process. Whatever that process may be, during any rehearsal period it is the actor's job to layer the journey of their character into the world of the play and the particular demands of the production.

Working with an accent adds another layer that will need to be woven into this process. It can be quite a delicate juggling act and one that will need careful consideration. On the one hand you don't want the accent to get in the way of your ability to focus, but on the other hand you want to be sure the accent is an integral part of the character. And of course, by the time you are in front of an audience you want the accent to be bedded in and authentic.

There is a lot to consider, and each of us finds our own way through, so here are some handy hints for getting the most out of yourself and your accent.

ACCENT MEETS DIRECTOR

You may work with some very different directorial approaches. We have known directors who:

● **Want you to speak all the time in the accent when in the rehearsal room.**
   This can be heaven or hell. Experience tells us that at its worst this approach will ingrain bad habits which become fixed and difficult to correct. At best, however, it can be an opportunity to make an accent feel as natural as your own speech. If this is what your director wants, you will need to be *very* disciplined. Whenever you are using the accent you are effectively working on it. It is tough to have to concentrate this hard on the accent all day, every day.

- **Don't want you to use the accent for the first week.**

  This is a very popular approach with directors. Be sure that you use your home time well to work on the accent and the text, as once they do ask you to use it they will expect the accent to be great! (See 'Get Practising', page 167.)

- **Wish they didn't have to deal with the accent at all!**

  This is the director that doesn't want to know about the accent, has had bad experiences with dialect coaches, or has seen good actors go bad simply because of the accent! Well, that's a tricky one: you will have to work independently and not expect any support. Try not to be dispirited by this and don't take it personally.

- **Want to give you accent notes.**

  Be grateful for the interest but know that they may not be the most sensitive or helpful remarks! If you are lucky enough to have a coach working on the show make sure you explain what your director has asked for so that together you can solve whatever problems arise.

Every director is unique, as is every actor, so whatever is happening make sure you are taking responsibility for yourself and your accent work. Look at 'Get Practising' (page 167) to find suggestions for structured ways of working. The one thing we can say for certain is that you *cannot* start work on the accent too soon!

ACCENT MEETS REHEARSAL

Always warm up your accent before rehearsals begin. It can take a good ten minutes of talking in an accent before you are fully engaged with it.

Of course, in rehearsal you are two people, yourself and the character ('You and the New'):

- When you are yourself, talking as yourself, it helps to have a 'springboard sentence' to get back into the accent when the scene starts again (see 'Springboard sentence', page 167).

- When you are in character, but not actually speaking, maybe you are pausing, thinking, relaxing, or listening in a scene, **don't relax out of the muscular setting** of the accent! Remember, the setting of the accent *is* the relaxed setting of your character's face. Likewise, if you 'uhm' and 'erm' the sound you hear should be the hesitation sound of the accent, not your own.

7

If you have time between scenes when you are not called, you can use it to listen to your resource recording and practise your accent on or off script. If your accent is getting in the way of your work in a scene it is a clear sign that you need to do more work outside rehearsals. During the rehearsal of a scene is *not* the time to do this kind of work.

> **TOP TIP**
> *It may be a good idea to record the rehearsal so that you can listen to it later and notice where you are making mistakes. It can also help to have an 'accent buddy' in the cast who you can ask to give you feedback on particular sounds or scenes that you are struggling with. Whatever you do, don't think that because you are using the accent all the time you don't need also to work on the specifics in a structured, focused way: you do!*

ACCENT MEETS CHARACTER

Age, gender, class, profession, family background and personal aspirations will all make a difference to the way someone sounds. Whatever acting process you have, connect your accent study to your character study.

Some actors use the following exercise to develop a character history/profile and it can also be a great way of getting to know the manner in which your character communicates.

● What do I say about other people?

● What do others say about me?

When you have answered those questions by looking through your script, find qualities within the accent that will help you portray them. Knowing the variety of 'T' formations in a London accent, for example, combined with little shifts in tune, can be great for conveying various emotional subtexts: 'Pass the bu?er, mum' (neutral); 'Pass the bu**dd**er, mum' (ingratiating); 'Pass the bu**tt**er, mum' (aggressive)! The same person can and will use all three varieties, depending on how they feel. If your character is given to being more aggressive or pushy, you will know which one to use!

On the other hand, you may think of the accent you are using as 'friendly', 'warm' and 'cuddly' but your character is referred to by others as 'spiteful', 'short-tempered' and 'cold'. Try to figure out what qualities within the accent can help you to portray these qualities. It may be in the groove or the consonant quality or simply the pace of delivery.

> *Jan was working on the RSC production of* Merry Wives the Musical. *One of the characters is called Pistol, so named because of his swaggering quick-fire repartee. The director wanted the actor playing Pistol to do a cockney accent. Using the punchy rhythms within the accent helped the actor find the much-needed personality traits of his character. Remember, the accent can serve the character. If you get to know the accent inside out you will see what it has to offer and how best to utilise it!*

If you can find a buddy, 'hot-seat' each other in the accent. This helps you to develop spontaneity and inner connection.

ACCENT MEETS AUDITION

You may have two weeks to prepare for an audition or you may have two days. You may be asked for a speech, or you may be asked to sight-read.

Ask yourself this question: **'How good am I at this accent?'** (be honest with yourself). Only then you can assess how much work you have to do and how much time you have to do it in.

There is always time to do something useful, even if you only have a day:

- Find a recording of the accent somewhere (see 'Making your own resource recording' (page 23) for ideas).
- Establish the Foundations (page 27).
- Check though the 'Major Players', especially the R (page 57) and the L (page 66).
- Get a sense of the 'Big Picture' groove (page 151).
- Decide on a couple of key vowel sounds.
- Find a 'springboard sentence' (page 167) to get you into the accent.

The more time you have, the more detail you can go into.

On the day

Before you go into the casting/audition make sure you have warmed the accent up, that you've got your springboard sentence and that the accent is ready to be switched on. It is a tall order to expect to be able to pull it out of the bag the moment you open your mouth.

If it is a sight-reading audition (aagghhh!), the assumption is that you can do the accent. You must have said you can or you wouldn't be there in the first place. The chances are they will give you the text to look at just before you go in. Make sure you get what you do know of the accent into your system: read the script out loud; get it into your mouth and body; feel the muscularity, the zone and the energy and direction of flow. Remember: the purpose of sight-reading is to demonstrate your talents as an *actor* and your suitability for the role. Focus on your acting and script skills. The odd mistakes in an accent will be forgiven if you have shown willing and are acting with integrity.

Don't forget to act!

Even a polished accent can have its downside. Actors can get carried away by the sound of the accent and forget some of the most basic acting prerequisites such as: listen and respond; be in the moment; connect to the impulse; remember what you want; etc.

If they give you the script in advance, here are some basic **script-skills** that don't take long and are invaluable to keep you connected to the drive of the text:

● Notice sentence lengths, punctuation, odd word use, etc.

● Mark the important/significant words.

● Mark the word at the end of each phrase and head towards it. The last word is so much more important than the first in terms of connection.

● Mark crescendos and changes of gear. Know the journey that your feelings and thoughts will move in.

While reading:

● Slow down your breathing. The most common mistake is to go too fast!

● Don't worry *at all* about being perfect. Be as good as you are. No better, no worse.

Finally, remember, they are interested in you as an *actor*, and will be more interested in an intelligent, professional approach to the accent and the acting. Having someone with potential is more important than having someone polished.

8

USEFUL STUFF

8

IN THIS CHAPTER

Making a Resource Recording:

- KIT LIST
- The Set Text ('Arthur the Rat')
- Major Player Elicitation sentences
- Free Speech prompts

You and the New Charts

- An example of one we did earlier!
- A blank chart for you to fill in

Knowing your Equipment

- Lips and Cheeks
- Jaw
- Tongue
- Soft Palate
- Voice Box

Space Exploration

- Vowel Spectrum chart
- Exploration and discovery of the eight extreme vowels

WHAT HAPPENS NEXT?

Congratulations! You have navigated your way around all the structures and processes of accents! Phew! You have developed new muscular awareness, you have expanded your flexibility and above all you have learned the architecture of accents.

At the very beginning of this book we said, 'Acting with an accent can be a dream or a nightmare for an actor', and in some ways this book may have had moments of both for you. Along with all the 'Well I never!', 'Who'd a thunk it?' moments you may well have had some nightmarish, 'What the @@**?', 'I just don't get it!' moments too. Don't despair. Contained within this book are *all* the tools you need to create honest, authentic connected accents. Some of the tools will act like instant coffee, while others may need percolating a little longer. Keep dipping in, revisiting, exploring, and bit by bit, through a combination of understanding the processes and putting them into practice, you can teach both your brain and your body how to do accents.

The advantages are huge. No more flailing around in the dark hoping you know what you're doing. No more going to dialect coaches wishing you knew more so that you can understand what they are saying! You now have a structure that you can apply to any accent.

The points of change from one accent to another may be many or few, but they can all be found within this basic architecture:

- Foundations
- Two Planets
- The Bite
- The Shapes
- The Groove.

What follows next are all the extras:

- Everything you need to make a resource recording: the KIT LIST, the questions to get your speakers talking, the Major Player elicitation sentences and the Set Text (pages 179–81).
- Example charts filled in with two contrasting accents (pages 182–91).
- You and the New charts (pages 192–201).
- Knowing your Equipment: the lips and cheeks, jaw, tongue, soft palate and voice box (pages 202–7).

8

- A full size vowel spectrum chart for charting your own and any new vowels you hear (page 208).
- Space Exploration pages for fuller exploration of your vowel space (pages 210–17).

MAKING A RESOURCE RECORDING

The KIT LIST ────────────────────────────

1	KIT		13	CLOTH
2	DRESS		14	THOUGHT
3	STRUT		15	NORTH
4	FOOT		16	FORCE
5	GOOSE		17	FACE
6	FLEECE		18	GOAT
7	NURSE		19	PRICE
8	TRAP		20	CHOICE
9	BATH		21	MOUTH
10	PALM		22	NEAR
11	START		23	SQUARE
12	LOT		24	CURE

(NB: In his book *Accents of English: An Introduction* (Cambridge University Press, 1982), the originator of the KIT LIST, J C Wells, includes a series of **KIT LIST sets** – a long list of words, subdivided into groups, whose vowels in Standard English and Standard American share the same sounds as the vowels in the 24 words above. An adapted and expanded version of Professor Wells' sets can be found on the *How to Do Accents* website, at **www.howtodoaccents.com/kitlistsets**.)

8

SET TEXT: ARTHUR THE RAT

There was once a young rat named Arthur, who could never take the trouble to make up his mind. Whenever his friends asked him if he would like to go out with them, he would only answer, 'I don't know.' He wouldn't say 'yes' and he wouldn't say 'no' either. He could never learn to make a choice.

His aunt Helen said to him, 'No one will ever care for you if you carry on like this. You have no more mind than a blade of grass.' Arthur looked wise, but stupidly said nothing.

One rainy day, the rats heard a great noise in the loft where they lived. The pine rafters were all rotten in the middle, and at last one of the joists had given way and fallen to the ground. The walls shook and all the rats' hair stood on end with fear and horror. 'This won't do,' said the old rat who was chief, 'I'll send out scouts to search for a new home.'

Three hours later the seven tired scouts came back and said, 'We have found a stone house, which is just what we wanted; there is room and good food for us all. There is a kindly horse named Nelly, a cow, a calf, and a garden with flowers and an elm tree.' Just then the old rat caught sight of young Arthur. 'Are you coming with us?' he asked. 'I don't know,' Arthur sighed. 'The roof may not come down just yet.' 'Well,' said the old rat angrily, 'we can't wait all day for you to make up your mind. Right about face! March!' And they went straight off.

Arthur stood and watched the other little rats hurry away. The idea of an immediate decision was too much for him. 'I'm going back to my hole for a bit,' he said to himself dreamily, 'just to make up my mind.' That Tuesday night there was a great crash that shook the earth and down came the whole roof. Next day some men rode up and looked at the ruins. One of them moved a board and hidden under it they saw a young rat lying on his side, quite dead, half in and half out of his hole.

We have updated **ARTHUR THE RAT** in order to include some extra vowel collisions and consonant clusters in the text.

Major Player elicitation sentences ————————

- **R:** Margaret, Linda and Gerry asked Peter if Roland started with 'R'.
- **L:** Larry the silly lamb slept peacefully in the field until hailstones fell.
- **H:** Harry Hobson had a holiday in Hawaii.
- **NG:** The singer was singing for the king.
- **TH:** That's my brother with a thermos of Matthew's broth.

Questions to get your speakers talking ————————

- What food do you most miss from home?
- What sort of scenery and landscape do you have in your area?
- What's your ideal home?
- What music do you like/dislike?
- What qualities do you value in a friendship?
- What 'bad habits' do you dislike in a person?
- How do you think your accent is perceived by others?
- What was your favourite childhood game/toy?

8

YOU AND THE NEW CHART – EXAMPLE

	ACCENT
YOU	London (East London)
NEW	Standard American

The Foundations (page 27)

	ZONE	TONE	SETTING AND HESITATION	DIRECTION
YOU	3	Brass Band	Jaw feels held Lips are flat and thin Soft Palate low 'aam'	Punched up onto the hard palate and then drives forward onto the teeth but stays there bit like getting trapped behind the tube doors!
NEW	4	Full, slight twang, bit of a honk bit like a duck	Jaw close together Lips are flat Energy in the cheeks Soft palate low	Think of surround speakers in the back of the head to get full oral and back of nose resonance then drive the sound forward and wide in the mouth

The Two Planets (page 41)

	RHOTIC	NON-RHOTIC	
		+Linking bounce	+Intrusive bounce
YOU	No	yes	yes
NEW	Yes	No	NO

The Bite (pages 55–112)

Major Players (page 57)

Pattern	R	L	NG	TH	H
	1 Tap 2 Bunch 3 Curl 4 Bend 5 Substitute	1 Only Light L 2 Only Dark L 3 Light and Dark L 4 Light L and W Sub	1 Hard in NG and ING words 2 Soft in NG and ING words 3 Hard In NG words and dropped in ING words 4 Soft in NG words and dropped in ING words	1 Standard everywhere 2 Plosive everywhere 3 T/D Substitutes everywhere 4 *D* at the start of a word, but *V* in the middle and end. *Voiceless*: Changes to *F* everywhere. 5 *Voiced*: **dropped** at the start of a word and *V* in the middle and end. *Voiceless*: *F* everywhere	Drop or not?
YOU	5	4	4	5	yes
NEW	2 (molar R)	2	2	1	no

Major Issues:

Voice Place Manner (page 88)

	VOICE	PLACE	MANNER
YOU	I have a breathy 'd' sound ie: in today and bad, the 'd' sounds like a 't'	The tip of my tongue sits down behind my bottom teeth on t/d/n/s/ sounds	my p/t/k are breathy feels like I use a lot of friction
NEW	T becomes voiced when it's in the middle of the word, such as better to bedder	The tongue tip and blade spreads out along the gum ridge	nothing obvious

8

The Glottal Stop (page 95)

	replace a T	accompany a T, P or K	replace an F or TH
YOU	always	Yes a lot of the time	'To' With a glottal
NEW	No	No	No

Collisions: Dropping and Crunching (page 101)

	CRUNCHING			DROPPING
	DY / TY / STY	DR / TR / STR	Any others?	Make a note of any drops you notice!
YOU	DY = joo TY = choo Sty + Shtoo	DR = jr TR = chr STR = Shtr	I do this alot IE What do you want wochoo wamp	Most =mos wept = we I miss off ends of words
NEW	DY = doo TY = too STY = stoo	No crunching	want to = wanna what do = wadda (what do, not what to)	/t /at the ends of words. use the tongue to form sound, but don't release it

YOOs (page 108)

	YOOS everywhere	Dropped after L and S	Dropped after L and S Crunched after T and D	Dropped after *all* gum-ridge consonants: S Z N T D L and THs
YOU			Drop and crunch	
NEW				Drop

The Shapes (pages 113–48)

Kit List (page 115)

	YOU	NEW
KIT	**I** It feels <u>short</u> and punchy quite close to i on the spectrum	**I** <u>Short</u>, it feels more relaxed, very slight 'uh' on the end.
DRESS	**ɛ** <u>Short</u>. It feels near to the 'e' on the spectrum.	**ɛ** <u>Short</u>, though a little longer than mine. And feels a little closer to '**a**'.
STRUT	**ʌ** <u>Short</u> UH – quite open, slight A sound to it.	**ʌ** <u>Short</u> UH – basically the same...maybe a little less open.
FOOT	**ʊ** <u>Short</u>. Lip pouts a tiny bit.	**ʊ** <u>Short</u>, not very different from mine.
GOOSE	**əu** <u>Sliding</u>. Long I've got a tiny schwa before the /oo/ vowel. My lips start relaxed and then round a tiny bit.	**uː** <u>Steady</u>. Long. Soft round lips. Sound feels further back.
FLEECE	**əi** <u>Sliding</u>. I start from UH in the centre and then slide to EE	**iː** <u>Steady and long</u>. Feels it very close to I on the spectrum.

8

Kit List (continued)

	YOU	NEW
NURSE	**ɜː** <u>Long, steady.</u> Feel my lips pout a bit.	**ɜˑ** <u>Long and steady</u> but it just feels like a molar R on its own!
TRAP	**æ** <u>Short</u>, close to my DRESS sound.	**æ** <u>Short.</u> Doesn't feel any different!
BATH	**ɑː** <u>Long, steady.</u> My lips round a bit, jaw open. Feel it at the back.	**æ** Seems the same as the TRAP vowel to me.
PALM	**ɑː** Same as BATH.	**ɑː** <u>Long and steady.</u> Same as mine!
START	**ɑː** Same as BATH and PALM	**ɑɹ** Vowel feels the same as PALM but I need to add the R, and start it while I'm doing the vowel.
LOT	**ɒ** <u>Short.</u> My jaw is open, I feel my cheeks come in a bit and my lips round a bit.	**a** <u>Short and steady.</u> Like my BATH vowel.

Kit List (continued)

	YOU	NEW
CLOTH	ɒ Same as LOT.	ɑ Feels the same as LOT.
THOUGHT	ɔu <u>Sliding</u> Cheeks pull in, lips round and then tighten.	ɑ Seems the same as LOT and CLOTH.
NORTH	As above.	ɔr Same as my THOUGHT vowel but with an added molar r.
FORCE	As above.	As above.
FACE	æi <u>Sliding</u>. It feels close to **a** on the spectrum and ends in i. I hit the first half and jump quickly to the second half.	ɛi <u>Sliding</u>. It starts closer to 'e' on the spectrum and ends in 'i' – ee. It feels equal on both halves and moves smoothly.
GOAT	ʌʊ <u>Sliding</u> I drop my jaw open and then close it with a little bit of lip-rounding.	ou <u>Sliding</u> Feels like one sound. Starts round and then rounds even more.

8

Kit List (continued)

	YOU	NEW
PRICE	**ɑɪ** <u>Sliding</u> Starts where my BATH vowel is and then my tongue bounces to my KIT vowel. Lips tighten across teeth.	**aɪ** <u>Sliding</u> Starts nearer the TRAP vowel and glides smoothly to their FLEECE vowel. Equal glide.
CHOICE	**ɔɪ** <u>Sliding</u> Starts at my THOUGHT and ends at FLEECE. Jumps from one to the other.	**ɔɪ** <u>Sliding</u> Same shapes but a smooth glide from one to the other.
MOUTH	**æː** <u>Long and Steady</u> Just like my TRAP vowel but long.	**aʊ** <u>Sliding</u> A smooth glide from TRAP vowel to FOOT vowel.
NEAR	**ɪː** <u>Long and steady</u> version of my KIT vowel. (Unless I'm cross then it's 'eeyuh'!)	**ɪr** It feels like it starts with the KIT vowel then I have to add molar r.
SQUARE	**eː** <u>Long</u> version of my DRESS vowel, with a very slight slide to UH at the end.	**er** It's their DRESS vowel with a molar r added.
TOUR (CURE)	**ɔː** Like my THOUGHT vowel.	OO then an a followed by an r

Main Inventory Issues (page 116)

	STRUT – FOOT One vowel or two?	FOOT – GOOSE – MOUTH One, two, or three vowels?	LOT – THOUGHT One vowel or two?	PRICE – CHOICE One vowel or two?
YOU	2	3	2	2
NEW	2	3	1	2

'R' Words (page 118)

For RHOTIC accents note the vowel that precedes the R (eg START takes TRAP vowel in our Southern Irish example). For NON-RHOTIC accents note the vowel that replaces the R (eg NORTH takes the THOUGHT vowel in our Standard English example).

	NURSE	START	NORTH	FORCE
YOU	no	no	no	no
NEW	Yes – it's only an R with no vowel shape	Yes – feels a bit like a LOT vowel	Yes – my vowel followed by R	Yes – my vowel followed by R

Main Distribution Issues (page 119)

Which vowel shape goes with which word in these sets?

	TRAP	BATH	PALM	START
YOU	Short A	Long AH	Long AH like BATH	Long AH like BATH
NEW	Shortish A, longer than mine tho'	Shortish A like TRAP	Long AH bit rounder than mine	Long AH Like PALM but with R

	LOT	CLOTH	THOUGHT	NORTH
YOU	Round short, jaw open	Exactly the same as LOT	Longish, lips very rounded	Exactly like THOUGHT
NEW	Open AH, like my BATH	Open AH	Open AH	Like mine but with R

8

	NEAR	SQUARE	CURE
YOU	no	no	no
NEW	Yes – KIT vowel followed by R	Yes – DRESS vowel followed by R	Yes – my THOUGHT vowel followed by R

Environmental Issues (page 141)

	NASAL COLOURING	R COLOURING	L EFFECT	UNSTRESSED ENDINGS		
				happY	commA	lettER
YOU	yes	no	I use two different vowels in goat and goal	fleece	opens towards A	Same as comma
NEW	yes	the r wraps itself tight around the vowel	No	fleece	a little less open and feels further back	Molar r

The Groove (page 149)

	LABAN ACTION	NEUTRAL Under or Over?	QUALITY? Major or Minor?
YOU	punchy	over	major
NEW	press	over	major

Specific Intonation Notes

<table>
<tr><td></td></tr>
<tr><td></td></tr>
<tr><td></td></tr>
</table>

<table>
<tr><td></td></tr>
<tr><td></td></tr>
<tr><td></td></tr>
</table>

Any other notes and observations…

American drives through to the end of the line. More words are stressed. It's a lot more direct. More stress on the personal pronoun.

8

YOU AND THE NEW CHART

	ACCENT
YOU	
NEW	

The Foundations (pages 27–38)

	ZONE	TONE	SETTING AND HESITATION	DIRECTION
YOU				
NEW				

The Two Planets (page 41)

	RHOTIC	NON-RHOTIC	
		+Linking bounce	+Intrusive bounce
YOU			
NEW			

The Bite (pages 55–112)

The Major Players (page 57)

Pattern	R	L	NG	TH	H
	1 Tap 2 Bunch 3 Curl 4 Bend 5 Substitute	1 Only Light L 2 Only Dark L 3 Light and Dark L 4 Light L and W Sub	1 Hard in NG and ING words 2 Soft in NG and ING words 3 Hard In NG words and dropped in ING words 4 Soft in NG words and dropped in ING words	1 Standard everywhere 2 Plosive everywhere 3 T/D Substitutes everywhere 4 *D* at the start of a word, but *V* in the middle and end. *Voiceless*: Changes to *F* everywhere. 5 *Voiced*: **dropped** at the start of a word and *V* in the middle and end. *Voiceless*: *F* everywhere	Drop or not?
YOU					
NEW					

Major Issues:

Voice Place Manner (page 88)

	VOICE	PLACE	MANNER
YOU			
NEW			

8

The Glottal Stop (page 95)

	replace a T	accompany a T, P or K	replace an F or TH
YOU			
NEW			

Collisions: Dropping and Crunching (page 101)

	CRUNCHING			**DROPPING**
	DY / TY / STY	DR / TR / STR	Any others?	Make a note of any drops you notice!
YOU				
NEW				

YOOs (page 108)

	YOOs everywhere	Dropped after L and S	Dropped after L and S Crunched after T and D	Dropped after **all** gum-ridge consonants: S Z N T D L and THs
YOU				
NEW				

The Shapes (pages 113–48)

Kit List (page 115)

	YOU	NEW
KIT		
DRESS		
STRUT		
FOOT		
GOOSE		
FLEECE		

Kit List (continued)

	YOU	NEW
NURSE		
TRAP		
BATH		
PALM		
START		
LOT		

Kit List (continued)

	YOU	NEW
CLOTH		
THOUGHT		
NORTH		
FORCE		
FACE		
GOAT		

Kit List (continued)

	YOU	NEW
PRICE		
CHOICE		
MOUTH		
NEAR		
SQUARE		
TOUR (CURE)		

Main Inventory Issues (page 116)

	STRUT – FOOT One vowel or two?	FOOT – GOOSE – MOUTH One, two, or three vowels?	LOT – THOUGHT One vowel or two?	PRICE – CHOICE One vowel or two?
YOU				
NEW				

Main Distribution Issues (page 118)

Which vowel shape goes with which word in these sets?

	TRAP	BATH	PALM	START
YOU				
NEW				

	LOT	CLOTH	THOUGHT	NORTH
YOU				
NEW				

'R' Words (page 119)

For RHOTIC accents, make a note of the vowel that precedes the R (eg START takes TRAP vowel in our Southern Irish example). For NON-RHOTIC accents note the vowel that replaces the R (eg NORTH takes the THOUGHT vowel in our Standard English example).

	NURSE	START	NORTH	FORCE
YOU				
NEW				

8

'R' Words (continued)

	NEAR	SQUARE	CURE
YOU			
NEW			

Environmental Issues (page 141)

	NASAL COLOURING	R COLOURING	L EFFECT	UNSTRESSED ENDINGS		
				happY	commA	lettER
YOU						
NEW						

The Groove (page 149)

	LABAN ACTION	NEUTRAL Under or Over?	QUALITY? Major or Minor?
YOU			
NEW			

Specific Intonation Notes

Any other notes and observations…

8

KNOWING YOUR EQUIPMENT

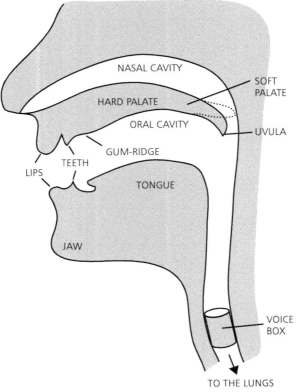

The articulators divide into two groups:

Passive (non-moving)

1 **Teeth**

2 **Upper gum-ridge**

3 **Hard palate**

Active (moving)

1 **Lips/cheeks**

2 **(Lower) Jaw**

3 **Tongue**

4 **Soft palate**

You will need a mirror so you can see what we are talking about!

The non-movable or **Passive articulators** are the ones you're just stuck with (unless you have surgery…). Using your tongue, explore the *passive* articulators and connect what you feel to the diagram.

It is the passive articulators that provide the structures against which the **Active articulators** play. The *active* articulators are the ones that do all the work.

Using the mirror, explore your *active* articulators:

1 LIPS and CHEEKS:

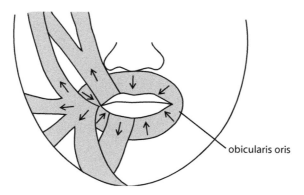

obicularis oris

The muscles of the lips and cheeks are interconnected.

Your **lips** have one principal muscle called the *orbicularis oris*. This muscle divides into *inner* and *outer sphincter* actions. When you use the outer sphincter your lips can round like this:

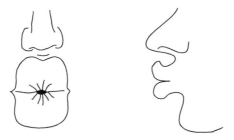

and when you use the inner sphincter they round like this:

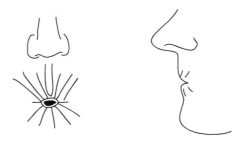

Some accents prefer one of these actions above another. Some like to make a proper circle, using a lot of rounding, while some use almost no rounding at all. Your **cheeks** have three principal muscle groups which pull the mouth in various directions:

- **sideways** into smiles, grins, etc
- **downwards** into a grimace
- **upwards** into sneers.

8

Try making these faces to see and feel these muscles at work. One or other of these muscles may be habitually loose or tight, active or passive in an accent.

2 JAW:

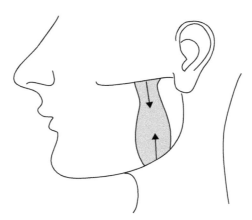

The lower jaw is attached to the upper jaw by muscle and ligament. To find this muscle, clench your teeth as if you are biting something with your back teeth. As you do this, put your fingers on your cheeks, just in front of your ears. You will feel the jaw muscle (the masseter) bunching. Try to picture how much space you have between your top and bottom teeth at the back as you sit at rest. The larger the space (without pulling), the looser the muscle. The jaw muscle holds different degrees of tension and looseness in different individuals and different accents.

3 TONGUE:

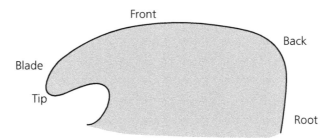

The tongue is a surprisingly large organ. It is probably bigger than you think. It often surprises people that the entire body of muscle, right down to the underside of the chin, is in fact your tongue. Feel under your chin with your thumb while you push your tongue up against the roof of your mouth. What you feel pushing down against your thumb is your tongue! Look at your tongue in the mirror. It's a bit like a separate creature living in your mouth. In fact, it is probably the most flexible and sensitive muscle in the human body. Look in the mirror to see the different sections of your tongue. To begin with, notice that your tongue divides into two main sections: a 'free' section and an 'attached' section. Look under the tongue and you will see the bit where it attaches to the jaw. This free section is the most flexible bit and is sub-divided into the **Tip** and the **Blade**. This tends to be the bit of the tongue we are most aware of. The attached section is the bit you probably overlook. This part of the tongue is sub-divided into the **Front**, **Centre**, **Back** and **Root**. The tongue will have areas of tension and looseness developed through the habitual movements of the language and accent it makes.

4 SOFT PALATE:

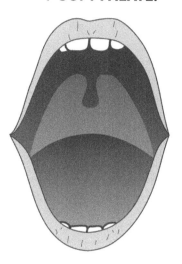

If the front of your tongue is super-flexible, you can feel your way back along the roof of your mouth, curling your tongue back on itself until you feel a ridge. That is the end of the hard palate and the beginning of the soft palate. Get a mirror, and look at the little punch bag that dangles in the back of your mouth (you'll need to get the light in the right place to see inside). That's your **Uvula**. It hangs from the very end of the soft palate. (You can stun someone at a party with that piece of information!) The job of the soft palate is to direct the breath or voice into either the nose or the mouth. In some accents, such as Manchester and Essex, the soft palate is held low, giving the sound a lot of 'nasal spill'; in some, such as West Ireland and North Yorkshire it is high, creating a more oral sound; while in others, such as a Neutral Standard English Accent, it has to bounce gymnastically up and down. Look again at the picture on page 202 and you will see how it can open or close the passage to the nose. So you can see that having a flexible soft palate is essential in order to do accents.

- To see the soft palate *lift up* and close the passageway to your *nose*, make a yawn while keeping your tongue flat and forward in your mouth. You'll see the little punch bag shoot up and disappear. Make an 'AH' as you do this and feel the sound resonating in the mouth.

- To see it *drop down* and close the passageway to your *mouth*, open your mouth and say 'NG', the sound from the end of the word **sing**. You will see the back of the tongue and the soft palate come together and feel the sound resonating in the nose.

- To feel it *bounce* switch from the closed 'NG' to the yawned 'AH' in one action. If your soft palate is a bit sluggish, the 'AH' will end up in your nose! See if you can switch the direction of sound from your nose to your mouth. You may need to give it a bit of exercise to tone up that muscle!

So those are your **articulators**. But of course, they only form speech when they have something to play with, and that's where your voice box comes in...

5 VOICE BOX:

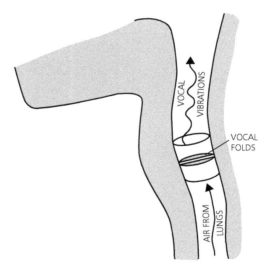

As the air leaves your lungs it passes through a piece of equipment called your **voice box** (also called the **larynx**). This 'box' contains two folds of flesh (**vocal folds**) that can either stay open to let air pass through unimpeded, or come together so that the outgoing air produces vibrations as it moves through them. You can see the voice box in the front of your neck. It's what a lot of us call the 'Adam's Apple'. Put your fingers on your neck and swallow and you will feel it bounce up and down. Men's voice-boxes are generally larger than women's and consequently they make lower notes.

To feel your voice vibrations 'switching on and off' try the following:

● Make a long 'V' and, without stopping the air flow, change it to an 'F'. You will feel the voice switch off.

● Reverse this: start with an 'F' and change it to a 'V'. You will feel the voice switch on.

● On one breath change from 'F' to 'V' a number of times. You will feel the voice switching on and off as the folds come together then apart, together, then apart.

You can do the same thing with an 'S' and 'Z' too. If you feel your face, neck and chest as you make voice vibrations you can feel the vibrations resonating. Speech sounds are made with both breath and voice vibrations. (You will often see this distinction described as 'voiced' and 'voiceless'.) Your articulators play with the air and vibrations in your mouth, holding them, diverting them, and shaping them to create the specific speech sounds of your language and accent.

So that's your bits!

Of course, the really clever thing is the way we move them about and bring them together. Make an 'FF' sound and you'll feel your top teeth contact your bottom lip. Add voice vibrations to this shape and the sound changes to a 'V'. Make a 'K' and you're feeling the back of the tongue lift up to contact the soft palate. Add voice vibrations and you're making a 'G'.

With all these moving parts, awareness and flexibility are the key to doing accents. This book will increase your flexibility as you explore new ways of playing with the sounds in your mouth. If you want to improve your basic voice use then it may help to invest in a good voice book such as *Finding Your Voice* by Barbara Houseman, or *The Voice Book* by Michael McCallion. (See 'Recommended Reading' in the Appendix, page 220.)

8

SPACE EXPLORATION

The Vowel Spectrum

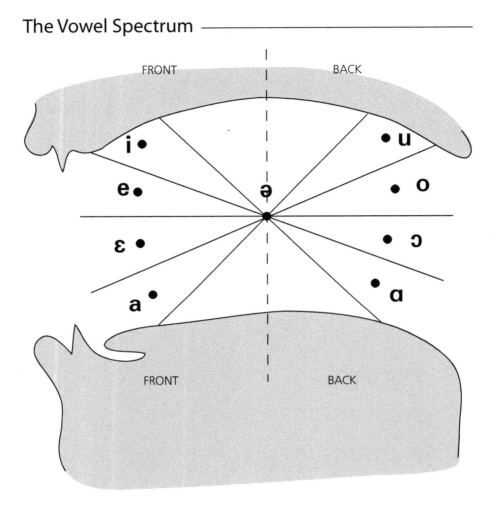

The aim of this section is to take your tongue into places it may never have been before and to give your tongue and ear new reference points.

We have put the extreme front vowels on TRACK 80 and the extreme back vowels on TRACK 82. Each vowel sound is repeated three times, followed by a short bleeping sound. After each bleep you will hear the next vowel sound.

As you move through these shapes and sounds some of them may be familiar. It may be that they are similar to vowels from your own accent. On the other hand you may find them all very odd. Think how many new sounds you will be shaping and hearing and the flexibility you will be developing as you explore!

Be specific with the movements and sounds: your speech muscles and your ear will get some things effortlessly whilst other shapes and sounds may take more focus and practice. Your brain may try to make shortcuts by using sounds and shapes it is familiar with.

Remember, this is about exploring *new* territory!

And don't panic! If you don't get it straight away, just keep listening, playing and exploring.

8

Mapping your mouth: the FRONT ——————

Preparation:

- Start with the jaw and tongue relaxed.
- The teeth should be a little apart with the tip of the tongue resting gently against the bottom front teeth.
- This places the tongue hump in the centre point of the map.
- The sound that goes with this is a small 'uh', called **neutral schwa.**

Exploration:

For each of the vowel shapes be sure to go through the following steps.

 Feel It: Read the instructions/descriptions of the shape and make the shape yourself, feeling the tongue move from neutral schwa and into the vowel shape.

 See It:

- Close your eyes and create a mind's eye picture of the shape you are making.
- Look at it in the mirror.
- Connect the way the shape looks and feels with the illustrations.

 Hear It: Breathe out through the shape on a whisper hearing the sound the shape makes.

Add Voice: When you can **feel it, hear it** and **see it,** fix the point in your *muscle memory* and *add voice* to it so that you can hear it fully, keeping the shape fixed and steady.

 Hear It and Compare It: Compare your sound to the sound on the track. If it doesn't sound the same, go back through the steps, adjust things as necessary, until the sound matches.

> **TOP TIP**
>
> *To do accents well, you need to train your mouth and ear to **feel** and **hear** how even subtle changes in the position of the lips and tongue can affect the sounds coming out of your mouth.*

Extreme Vowel One: i

For the first extreme vowel the hump in the tongue is at its highest and furthest forward in the mouth and the lips are very spread and the jaw is close together. The resonance this shape creates is very high frequency.

- **JAW**: Let your jaw open *just a little*.
- **LIPS**: Spread the lips.
- **TONGUE**: Keep the tip of your tongue down behind your bottom teeth. Squeeze the hump of your tongue up and forwards from the centre point and towards the roof of the mouth and the gum-ridge.

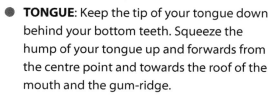

Follow the instructions in the shaded boxes on page 210 and focus the sound onto the gum-ridge.

- Listen to us make the sound three times.
  (Remember, after the bleep you will hear a new vowel sound.)
- The sound has an EE-like quality.
- This is your first extreme reference point.

Extreme Vowel Two: e

If you open the jaw just the tiniest bit from the first extreme position, keeping the tongue humping up and forward, and relaxing the lips just a little, you will find yourself making extreme vowel two! It sounds a little like the Scottish vowel in TAKE and the French vowel in THÉ (tea).

- **JAW**: Let the jaw open *one finger's drop*.
- **LIPS**: Keep the lips spread.

8

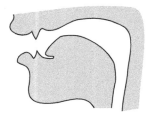

● **TONGUE**: Keep the tip of the tongue down behind your bottom teeth. Squeeze the hump of the tongue up towards the roof of your mouth and the gum-ridge, without closing the jaw.

Follow the instructions in the shaded boxes on page 210 and focus the sound on the front of your tongue.

● Listen to us make the sound.
● The sound has an EH-like quality.
● This is your second extreme reference point.

Extreme Vowel Three: ɛ

If you open the jaw a little more, keep the tongue humped up and forward you will find yourself making extreme vowel three.

● **JAW:** Let the jaw drop open *one and a half fingers' drop*.
● **LIPS:** Keep the lips spread just a little.
● **TONGUE:** Raise the hump of the tongue just a little towards the roof of your mouth and your gum-ridge, keeping the jaw open.

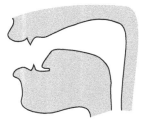

Follow the instructions in the shaded boxes on page 210 and focus the sound on the front of your tongue

● Listen to us make the sound.
● The sound has an EH-like quality.
● This is your third extreme reference point.

Extreme Vowel Four: a

For the last extreme reference point at the front of your mouth the jaw is fully open. The hump in the tongue is still towards the front and fairly low in the mouth. The lips are spread a tiny bit.

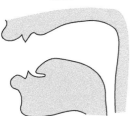

- **JAW:** Let your jaw drop fully open, around *two fingers' drop*.
- **LIPS:** Keep the lips slightly spead.
- **TONGUE:** Keep the tip of your tongue forward, resting against your bottom teeth and roll the body of the tongue gently up and forward *just a little* as if letting someone glimpse your tongue piercing!

Follow the instructions in the shaded boxes on page 210 and focus the sound on the front of the tongue.

- Listen to us make the sound.
- The sound has an A-like quality.
- That is your fourth extreme reference point.

… You're halfway there, but before you go on…

- By gliding from the top to the bottom and back again: **i–e–ɛ–a, a–ɛ–e–i**, passing through each of these points, you can hear and feel the rainbow of vowel possibilities at the front of your mouth.

- By adding lip-rounding to each of these tongue positions you will hear even more vowel possibilities! When you add lip-rounding to the **e** you can hear the French vowel in 'œuf', and when you round the **i** you will hear the Scots vowel in 'you'!

8

Mapping your mouth: the BACK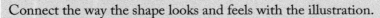

Preparation:

- Start with the jaw and tongue relaxed.
- The teeth should be a little apart with the tip of the tongue resting gently against the bottom front teeth.
- This places the tongue hump in the centre point of the map.
- The sound that goes with this is a small 'uh'.

Five stages of exploration:

For each of the vowel shapes be sure to go through the following steps.

 Feel It: Read the instructions/descriptions of the shape and make the shape yourself, feeling the tongue move from the centre point and into the vowel shape.

 See It: Close your eyes and create a mind's eye picture of the shape you are making. Look at it in the mirror.

Connect the way the shape looks and feels with the illustration.

 Hear It: Breathe out through the shape on a whisper hearing the sound the shape makes.

Add Voice: When you can **feel it**, **hear it** and **see it**, fix the point in your *muscle memory* and *add voice* to it so that you can hear it fully keeping the shape fixed and steady.

 Hear It and Compare It: Compare your sound to the sound on the track. If it doesn't sound the same, go back through the steps, adjust things as necessary, until the sound matches.

Extreme Vowel Five: ɑ

For the fifth extreme vowel the lips are now completely relaxed, the jaw is fully open and the hump in the tongue has moved to the back of the mouth.

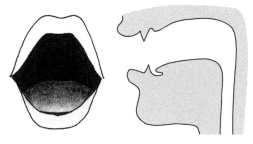

- **JAW:** Let your jaw drop fully open, around *two fingers' drop*.
- **LIPS:** Keep your lips soft (not spread!)

- **TONGUE:** Anchor the tip of your tongue gently behind your bottom teeth. Relax the front of your tongue. (Yawn ever so slightly to lift the soft palate.)

Follow the instructions in the shaded box on page 214 and focus the sound on the back of the tongue.

- Listen to us make the sound.
- The sound has an AH-like quality.
- This is your fifth extreme reference point.

Extreme Vowel Six: ɔ

For the sixth extreme vowel the lip-rounding begins!

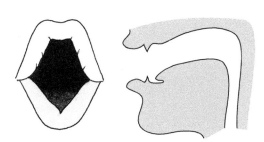

- **JAW:** Keep the jaw almost fully open, around *one and a half fingers' drop*.
- **LIPS:** Round the lips as in the illustration.

- **TONGUE:** Keep the tip of the tongue relaxed by the bottom front teeth. The back of the tongue rises towards the soft palate. (Yawn a little to lift the soft palate out of the way!)

Follow the instructions in the shaded box on page 214 and focus the sound on the back of the tongue.

- Listen to us make the sound.
- The sound has a quality like the vowel in OR.
- This is your sixth extreme reference point. *(Two more to go!)*

8

Extreme Vowel Seven: o

We're coming into the home straight now! For this extreme vowel the jaw closes a little and the lips round even more.

 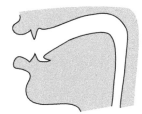

- **JAW**: Close the jaw to *one finger's drop.*
- **LIPS**: Round the lips leaving enough space for one finger.

- **TONGUE**: Keep the tip of the tongue relaxed by the bottom front teeth and raise the back of the tongue towards the soft palate.

Follow the instructions in the shaded box on page 214 and focus the sound on the back of the tongue.

- Listen to us make this sound on the track.
- The sound has an OH-like quality.
- This is your seventh extreme reference point. *(One more to go!)*

Extreme Vowel Eight: u

This is it, the final extreme vowel. For this one the lips are fully rounded and the back of the tongue is at its highest point in the mouth making a very low resonant frequency.

 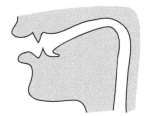

- **JAW**: Let the jaw drop open *just a little.*
- **LIPS**: Pull in the cheeks and round the lips as in the illustration.

- **TONGUE**: Keep the tip of the tongue down and raise the back of your tongue as close as possible to a G position without actually making a G!

Follow the instructions in the shaded box on page 214 and focus the sound on the back of the tongue.

- Listen to us make the sound.

How to Do Accents

- The sound has an OO-like quality.
- That is your eighth and final extreme vowel!

… But before you make yourself a cuppa…

- By gliding from the bottom to the top and back again: **ɑ–o–ɔ–u, u–ɔ–o–ɑ,** passing through each of these points, you can hear and feel the rainbow of vowel possibilities at the back of your mouth.
- You can even glide from front to back at the top: **i–u**
- And front to back at the bottom: **a–ɑ**
- By adding and removing lip-rounding to each of these shapes you will hear even more possibilities!

Doing these explorations regularly will give your speech muscles and your ear the flexibility they need to be really good at accents.

8

APPENDIX

RECOMMENDED INTERNET RESOURCES

- **The ACCENT Kit app:**
  ios bit.ly/U9jZNL
  Android bit.ly/12nSrIq
  http://theaccentkit.com
  This App features recordings
  of authentic speakers of accents
  of English using the structure
  of Free Speech, Arthur the Rat
  (practice text) Foundations, Word
  List, Vowel Sentences and Major
  Players. Perfect for use with this
  book!

- **http://accent.gmu.edu**
  The Speech Accent Archive is a
  project of the Center for History
  and New Media. It presents a large
  set of speech samples from a variety
  of language backgrounds. Native
  and non-native speakers of English
  read the same paragraph and are
  carefully transcribed.

- **www.bbc.co.uk**
  This is a good website generally.
  You can listen to interviews on
  Radio 4 and check out the excellent
  'Routes Of English' series that has
  some great samples and background
  information on accents and dialects
  of English. (You can in fact buy this
  series in book and CD form.)

- **www.bbc.co.uk/voices**
  The clips are drawn from the
  'Voices' recordings – which capture
  1,200 people in conversation.
  There's a great map that you can
  'hover' over to locate the samples
  you're looking for.

- **www.bl.uk/learning/langlit/**
  sounds
  www.collectbritain.co.uk/
  collections/dialects
  These are the British Library
  websites with some lovely archive
  recordings of British accents and
  dialects.

- **www.google.com /**
  www.google.co.uk
  Put in the name of the accent you
  are looking for together with the
  words 'accent' or 'dialect' and see
  what you get!

- **www.youtube.com**
  You will find people demonstrating
  their accents all over the place on
  this site, either deliberately or by
  default!

- **www.publicradiofan.com**
  This website lists all the
  international public radio stations,
  telling you which ones are currently
  online and giving live access.

- **http://web.ku.edu/idea**
  IDEA – the International Dialects
  of English Archive – is a Kansas
  University project; it is not,
  however, limited to American
  accents. We like it because it often
  offers more than one example and
  gives details of the gender, age,
  race and profession of the speakers.
  Each speaker reads a passage of text
  specifically written to contain all
  the possible sound combinations
  of English, as well as contributing
  some 'free conversational speech'.

RECOMMENDED READING

Voice and Speech books

Cicely Berry, *Voice and the Actor* (John Wiley and Sons, 1991)

Christina Gutekunst and John Gillett, *Voice into Acting* (Bloomsbury, 2014)

Barbara Houseman, *Finding Your Voice* (Nick Hern Books, 2002)

Malcolm Morrison, *Clear Speech* (A & C Black, 2001)

Michael McCallion, *The Voice Book* (Faber & Faber, 1998)

Phonetics and Phonology books

Patricia Ashby, *Speech Sounds* (Routledge, 2005)

Beverley Collins and Inger Mees, *Practical Phonetics and Phonology* (Routledge, 2003)

J C Wells, *English Intonation: An Introduction* (Cambridge University Press, 2006)

Accent books

Arthur Hughes, Peter Trudgill and Dominic Watt, *English Accents and Dialects* (Hodder Arnold, 2005)

Robert McCrum, William Cran and Robert MacNeil, *The Story of English* (Faber & Faber, 2002)

Melvyn Bragg, *The Adventure of English: The Biography of a Language* (Hodder & Stoughton, 2003)

J C Wells, *Accents of English* (three volumes; Cambridge University Press, 1982)

Jan Haydn Rowles & Edda Sharpe, *How To Do Standard English Accents* (Oberon Books, 2012)

INDEX OF REFERENCES TO ACCENTS IN THE BOOK

INDEX OF TRACK LISTS IN REFERENCE TO ACCENTS

MP3 FULL TRACK LISTING

The Foundations
01 The 7 Zones
02 Zoning (*Manchester, Cockney, NSEA*)
03 Settings
04 Hesitation Sounds

The Two Planets
05 Rhotic Speakers (*Glasgow, American, Belfast*)
06 Non-Rhotic Speakers (*Norfolk, South Wales, Newcastle*)
07 Mid-Word R (*Standard American, NSEA*)
08 Linking R (*Norfolk, Liverpool, Newcastle*)
09 Intrusive R (*Norfolk, Walsall, Yorkshire*)

Major Players: R
10 Gum-ridge Tap (*Liverpool*)
11 Retroflex Tap (*Punjabi*)
12 Uvular Tap (*Old Newcastle*)
13 Bunched Molar R (*Standard American*)
14 Curled Retroflex R (*Belfast*)
15 Bending Free R (*Southern Irish*)
16 R Substitute (*Cockney*)

Major Players: L
17 Light Ls (*South Wales*) Dark Ls (*Manchester*) Light/Dark Combination (*NSEA*) Light/Substitute Combination (*Essex*)
18 Light L's
19 Dark L's
20 Light/Dark Combination
21 Light/Substitute Combination

Major Players: H
22 *Newcastle, Cockney*
23 *Contemporary 'Street' London*

Major Players: NG
24 Hard NG (*Manchester*) Soft NG (*Essex*)

25 Dropped NG (*Norfolk, South Wales, Cockney, Canadian*)
26 The NG Patterns (all hard, all soft, soft NG + dropped ING)

Major Players: TH
27 TH Possibilities
28 Examples: *NSEA, Southern Irish, West Indian, Contemporary 'Street' London, Essex*
29 *Cockney*

Major Issues
30 Consonant Qualities
31 De-voicing (*Southern Irish*) Voicing (*Cornwall*)
32 Place of Contact (T/K)
33 Place of Contact (*Essex, NSEA, Punjabi*)
34 Manner of Release (*Liverpool/Manchester Glasgow/ Southern Irish*)
35 Aspiration + / (*Essex, Punjabi*)
36 Glottal Stop
37 Glottal Stops (*Norfolk, Newcastle, Cockney*)
38 Glottal Stop replaces T (*Norfolk*)
39 Glottal Stop accompanies T,P and K (*Newcastle*)
40 Glottal Stop replaces 'to' and 'the' (*Essex, Yorkshire*)
41 Dropped Consonants (*Cockney*)
42 Crunched Consonants (*Essex, Manchester, Glasgow*)
43 Crunched Consonants (*West Midlands*)
43a tn dn/tl dl
44 T with issues (*Cockney*)
45 Springing Consonants W R Y (*Manchester, Cockney, Belfast*)
46 Yoo Pattern 1 (*Old RP*)
47 Yoo Pattern 2 (*Yorkshire*)
48 Yoo Pattern 3 (*West Midlands*)

49 Yoo Pattern 4 (*Standard American*)
50 Yoo Special (*Wales*)
51 Yoo Special (*Norfolk*)

The Shapes
52 GOAT (*Glasgow, West Midlands*)
53 The Neutral Schwa
54 Extreme Vowels Voiced
55 Extreme Vowels Whispered
56 Adding and removing Lip-Rounding
57 Accent vowels on the Spectrum
58 Vowel Lengths (*Glasgow, Canada, Norfolk, Yorkshire*)
59 PRICE vowel: *S. Irish, Standard American, Cockney*
60 PRICE vowel: *Yorkshire, Berkshire*
61 PRICE: vowel: *Contemporary 'Street' London*
62 MOUTH vowel: *Dublin, Belfast, Essex*
63 GOAT/FACE vowels: *Glasgow, Yorkshire, Derbyshire, West Midlands, London*
64 GOAT/FACE vowels: *Standard American, West Indian*
65 NEAR/SQUARE/CURE: Stages of R Loss
66 GOOSE/FLEECE vowels: *South Wales, Cockney*
67 Environmental Issues: Nasalisation (*Essex, American*)
68 Environmental Issues: R Colouring (*Southern Irish, American*)
69 Environmental Issues: *L* Effect (*RP, NSEA, London*)
70 Environmental Issues: Free and Blocked (*Canadian*)
71 Unstressed Syllables: Schwa (*Liverpool, NSEA, Cockney*)

72 Unstressed Syllables (*Yorkshire/NSEA, NSEA/ Standard American*)
72a Vowel Clusters

The Groove
73 Contrastive Grooves
74 Laban Dynamics
75 Laban Dynamics in accents: *Standard American, Glasgow, Contemporary 'Street' London, Yorkshire, Swansea, Walsall, Essex, Cork.*
76 Default Tunes (*Liverpool/ NSEA*)
77 Intonation (*NSEA*)
78 Singing the Tune (*Belfast, Cockney*)
79 Intonation and Action (*NSEA*)

Appendix: Space Exploration
80 Extreme Front Vowels
81 Front Slides
82 Extreme Back Vowels
83 Back Slides

Sample Accents
(*Kit List, 'Arthur the Rat', Schwa, Free Speech*)
84 Norfolk
85 Yorkshire
86 Standard Canadian
87 Standard Australian
88 Standard American
89 Northern Irish (Belfast)
90 Southern Irish (Cork)
91 Scottish (Glasgow)
92 Newcastle
93 Manchester
94 Liverpool
95 South Wales (Swansea)
96 West Midlands (Walsall)
97 Cockney
98 Neutral Standard English
99 Contemporary 'Street' London
100 Cornish

TO DOWNLOAD THE MP3 RESOURCE PACK

To download the MP3 resource pack:

Open your internet browser and go to **www.oberonbooks.com/accents**

1. Click the download link in the middle of the page

2. A compressed zip file (HowToDoAccents.zip) will automatically begin downloading

3. Once it has finished, go to the designated download folder on your computer

4. Right click on HowToDoAccents.zip, and click 'Extract'

5. When prompted enter the password: **HTDA521**

6. This will open a folder named How To Do Accents Resource Pack, containing **100** audio MP3 files

7. Simply drag and drop or copy and paste these files to wherever you wish to store them on your computer

If you require any further technical support, please contact **info@oberonbooks.com** or telephone **+44 (0)207 607 3637**